WHEN I OPEN MY WINDOW

Reflections
for the
Living of these Days

To Hal and Barbara —

With gratitude for your
friendship — and wishing you
love, joy and peace for the
living of your days —

Tich

Cover Design
Martha Rowse Kelder

A Publication of
GRENFELL READING CENTER
36 Narramissic Drive
Orland, Maine 04472-0098
Tel. 1-207-469-7102
Email: clarine@aol.com

ISBN 0-9612766-8-1

Printed in the United States of America by
Furbush-Roberts Printing Co., Bangor, ME

WHEN I OPEN MY WINDOW

Reflections
for the
Living of these Days

Chandler W. Gilbert

Rev. Dr. Chandler 'Tuck' Gilbert

DEDICATION

This book is dedicated,
with love, respect and admiration,
to all who have taught and encouraged me
to open the windows
of my heart, my soul, and my mind,
especially
. . . to Bobbie, loving companion and wife
for nearly fifty years,
. . . to our daughters, Ann and Jane,
...to our son, Mark,
whose twenty years were
lived with astonishing courage,
an irrepressible sense of fun,
and an abounding love for life,
. . . and to a host of friends and parishioners
at First Congregational Church,
Westfield, Massachusetts,
and at Trinitarian Congregational Church,
United Church of Christ,
Concord, Massachusetts

CONTENTS

PREFACE

I. YEARNING FOR FAITH

II. ON BEING MORE FULLY ALIVE

III. WALKING THROUGH THE VALLEY OF THE SHADOW

IV. GROWING OLDER

V. RELATIONSHIPS

VI. RESPONSE ABILITY

PREFACE

This is a book for seekers -- I am a seeker, too.
This is also a book for doubters -- I am a doubter, too.
Finally, this is a book for believers -- I am a believer, too.

This book is a collection of short reflections or musings among which one may browse at random. Initially written for myself, I think of it now as having been written for all who walk some of the paths I walk. Many other minds and hearts have found their way into it. Some are acknowledged in the text, others in the final credits. I am grateful to each contributor, named and unnamed.

However, it is to you, my readers, that I am most grateful, for the reflections in **When I Open My Window** are open-ended, and I am counting on you to add your thoughts to mine and so complete this book.

The title, of course, refers to opening the window of one's heart, mind, soul and life. Sometimes the sounds that drift in my open window are of joy, beauty, or love; sometimes of sorrow, pain, or need. At other times they are simply the sounds of silence. I am inviting you, as you read, to listen to the sounds I have heard and then take time to listen and reflect on whatever sounds *you* are hearing.

You may find it helpful to approach this book in the spirit of a visitor browsing in an art gallery. Move slowly, stop where something beckons attention, then stroll on. Pause here, then there to contemplate. Then move on again, the only goal being to see, hear, listen and enjoy.

Although I am grateful to all who have encouraged me and contributed to the preparation of these pages, three deserve special mention -- Martha Rowse Kelder, Greg Lawn, and Clarine Coffin Grenfell.

Martha, in the reflective painting on the cover of this book, perfectly portrays my own vision of the open window. Greg Lawn, owner of Savron Graphics, has been both technical advisor and understanding friend in the final stages of producing this book. Clarine, formerly an editor in the Educational Division of **Reader's Digest,** since 1975 director of the Grenfell Reading Center, has done more than any other person to help this book find its way into print. Editor and publisher, she has also been patient teacher, genial taskmaster, and occasionally a much-needed cheerleader whose unfailing sense of humor has made the hard work fun. I count these three as valued friends and thank them with all my heart.

So -- seekers, doubters and believers, turn the pages, read the words, hear the sounds, then take time to reflect and respond. Know that I would be delighted to hear from you. Who knows? Perhaps my next book may be entitled, *Reflections of My Readers!*

'Tuck' Gilbert
Jaffrey, New Hampshire
Autumn, 2001

I. YEARNING FOR FAITH

The enterprise
Is exploration into God.
Christopher Fry,
in ***The Sleep of Prisoners***

My heart is restless until it finds its
rest in Thee, O God.
St. Augustine

As a deer longs for flowing streams,
so my soul longs for you, O God. My
soul thirsts for God, for the living God.
Psalm 42:1-2

CIRCLING AROUND GOD

Introducing Part I

There lives more faith in honest doubt,
Believe me, than in half the creeds.
Alfred, Lord Tennyson

My yearning for faith began in a religious home where God was central, Jesus was the window to God, and the Bible the key to both. My parents were missionaries to China, but should not be confused with those narrow, literalistic, pith-helmeted, Bible-thumping, self-righteous sorts too often portrayed by Hollywood or in novels such as *The Poisonwood Bible.* Nothing like that at all!

They and most of their colleagues were modern men and women, highly educated graduates of first-rate colleges such as Wesleyan, Bates, Harvard and Yale. They were idealistic, heroic, hard-working, world-changing, Christ-committed, faith-inspired. They were medical doctors, nurses, social workers, teachers, administrators, agriculturalists, and ministers. By today's standards, they were often moralistic. My sister, Mariel Kinsey, once described them as "strong women and staunch men who wore New England church spires up their backs!" There is some truth to that.

However, most of the missionaries I was privileged to know were far from stiff and solemn. I grew up surrounded by frequent laughter and hilarity, delectable picnics, and never-to-be-forgotten evening boat rides on the nearby canal, singing songs such as *My Bonnie Lies Over the Ocean, Pack Up Your Troubles in Your Old Kit Bag,* and *Pull Your Shades Down, Mary Ann.* In the summer, there were tennis tournaments, donkey polo games, and baseball competitions with sailors from the Pacific Fleet of the United States Navy. On summer evenings the large community of vacationing missionaries often gathered for picnics by the sea, the high point of which was the singing of hymns. As the sun set, we always sang *Day Is Dying in the West.* To this day I cannot sing that hymn without getting a lump in my throat.

My father, unswervingly loyal to Christ, made remarkable efforts to shape his life according to how he thought Jesus would have him live it. My mother, more the questioner, struggled with religious doubts throughout her life, feeling guilty and inadequate because she could not buy wholeheartedly into the faith that governed the lives of most of the adults around her. I followed in my father's footsteps professionally, but tended to walk more in my mother's when it came to matters of faith. When I left for my first parish, my mother wisely advised me to "religiously take a day off in as *unreligious* an atmosphere as possible!"

I have lived most of my life on what Jay Parini, one of Robert Frost's biographers, calls *"the perilous fault line between skepticism and faith."* I have had a great need to make sense of things, to make religious faith honest, credible, rational, understandable. Over the years, however, I have become less and less comfortable with my rationalism and have circled away from all that sense-making, attempting to lay hold of something more of the heart than of the head. I have learned to see that not all mysteries need to be solved, that, as Jelalludin Rumi puts it, *"the eye goes blind only when it insists on seeing why."* So I continue to walk that perilous fault-line, sometimes closer to skepticism, sometimes closer to faith. Often skeptical of my faith, I have learned to be equally skeptical of my doubts.

In short, for most of my adult life I have been circling around God. Sometimes God seems close, sometimes distant. During the times when God seems most distant, I feel like the teenager in one of my parishes who said, "I am homesick in my own home." That fifteen-year-old girl was missing some badly needed closer relationship with her parents. What has often been missing for me is a closer relationship with God. There are other times, however, when I experience closeness and *know* God's presence.

I am not alone in my experiences of a God who, at times, seems distant or absent. The Psalmists, for example, wrote an astonishing number of psalms about the absence of God and their yearning for a livelier sense of God's presence. Even the saints know what it is to be 'homesick for God.'

The writer of *Ecclesiastes* claims *"For everything there is a season...a time to be born, and a time to die; a time to plant, and a time to pluck up what is planted...."* (3:1 ff.) What a relief it would have been to me and vast numbers of others if he had added, "a time to be close to God, and a time to be distant from God, a time for faith, and a time for doubt."

That's what the reflections in this first section are about -- faith and doubt, closeness and distance, spiritual springtime and spiritual wintertime, seeking and finding.

* * *

NOTHING CAN SEPARATE US

God is not always silent, and man is not always blind. In every man's life there are moments when there is a lifting of the veil at the horizon of the known, opening a sight of the eternal. Each of us has at least once...experienced the momentous reality of God....The remembrance of that experience and loyalty to the response of that moment are the forces that sustain our faith....

Abraham Heschel
in *I Asked for Wonder*

Nothing ever becomes real until it is experienced.
John Keats

Our first child, a beautiful and vivacious little blonde, was one-and-a-half years old. In mid-winter her persistent runny nose and unusual paleness did not seem worrisome to us. We were not aware that our family doctor, a fellow church member, was vaguely uneasy about her. One Sunday morning while we were at worship, he wandered up to the Toddlers' Room and quietly observed her for a while. Something, he thought, did not seem right. After worship, he suggested we bring her in for another check-up. That office visit was the beginning of a nightmare. The examination and subsequent tests revealed a large, malignant growth in her abdomen.

The surgery was long and complicated. The tumor was wrapped around her aorta. Removing it was touch-and-go. A major nerve to her leg had to be severed. The surgeon, a man with sure hands, a large heart and a beautiful spirit, came down to the room where we had been waiting all those anxious hours to tell us what lay ahead. With tears in his eyes, he told us there would be intensive radiation for several weeks and that if she lived, she might never have the use of her leg. We were devastated. Visits to her in the hospital were unbelievably painful. Too young to understand either her illness or what must have seemed to her to be abandonment, she wailed uncontrollably each time we left.

The prolonged nightmare was the occasion for one of the most startling spiritual experiences either my wife or I have ever had. We had been to the hospital one evening and had come home particularly discouraged and heavy of heart. As I walked into our kitchen, I was suddenly overwhelmed with the absolute certainty that our little daughter was going to be okay. It was clear to me that okay did not necessarily mean that she would survive or ever be physically whole again. It simply meant that whether she lived or died, she would be all right. The burden was not gone, but I felt as if Something or Someone had lifted it. A tremendous sense of relief swept over me and a peace I had not known for many days, and for that matter had never before felt so strongly. I turned to Bobbie and said, "Something strange just happened to me," and told her about it as best I could. She said, "You won't believe this -- the same thing just happened to me."

At funerals and on other occasions, I had often read the words of Paul, *"I am convinced that neither death, nor life...nor things present, nor things to come...will be able to separate us from the love of God...."* (Romans 8:37-39) I had believed those words were true. Now I *knew*! As it turned out, our daughter did survive. She carries some ongoing physical after-effects, but is in good health, a wife, a mother, and, in our opinion, an exceptional human being.

I have had other memorable experiences of the immediate and powerful presence of God, but none as startling, persuasive and transformative as the one that happened to us in our kitchen forty-six years ago. Over all these years that experience has helped sustain me. Perhaps someday something like this will happen to me again. If it does, I imagine it will come out of the blue, not because I expect it or ask for it, but simply because I am open to it. Beyond that, the experience of God's presence is pure gift, amazing grace.

* * *

LOOK DOWN, NOT UP

The day of my spiritual awakening was the day I saw -- and knew I saw -- all things in God and God in all things.
Mechtild of Magdeburg

Raise the stone and thou shalt find me; cleave the wood and there am I.
Henry Van Dyke

Many years ago a friend of mine was hiking along a dirt road in Vermont. Up ahead, sitting on a stone wall, was a craggy-looking, white-haired man who looked from a distance like Robert Frost. As my friend drew near, he was elated to see that it really *was* the famous poet. As he tells the story, he ventured to engage Frost in conversation, and to his delight Frost seemed in a talkative mood. The dialogue eventually took a theological turn. "Do you believe in God?"my friend asked. "I'm not quite sure," Frost replied, "but one thing I know -- if you want to find Him, look down, not up."

I find myself increasingly impatient with a religious point of view that persists in separating body from soul, earthiness from spirituality, the God 'up there' from life 'down here.' Surely God is in the earthiness of body and in all the pungency of life in the here and now. In other words, "If you want to find God, look down, not up." That may not be the whole truth, but it is an essential part of it.

* * *

WHERE CAN I FIND GOD?

God is at home; it is we who have gone out for a walk.

Meister Eckhart

"I was passionate, filled with longing, I searched far and wide. But the day that the truthful One found me, I was at home."

Lal Dad, a 14th century Kashmir

People seek God in many ways and in many places. Some travel great distances to visit shrines and sacred places. Some go to workshops and retreats far from home. Some bounce from church to church looking for just the right place to get close to God. Some experiment with different denominations or religions. Some read voluminously, even obsessively, hoping to find some theologian, mystic or guru who will assuage their spiritual thirst.

From time to time I have been rescued from my yearning for God by discovering a voice that spoke what I needed to hear. At one point in my life, for example, Paul Tillich was my rescuer; at another, it was Teilhard de Chardin. Then along came Henri Nouwen, then Frederick Buechner, then Kathleen Norris, then Martin Marty. My list of rescuers is long and I am forever

17

grateful for all those whose insights have fed me just when I was hungriest. However, I am also grateful for reminders that sometimes my search for God can be satisfied closer to home, a point delightfully made clear by the following version of this classic tale:

Once upon a time there was a very devout rabbi by the name of Eisek. He lived in Cracow, at that time the capital of Poland. Rabbi Eisek had a dream. "Eisek," a voice said, "go on a journey to far-off Prague. There, under a bridge, you will discover a hidden treasure of very great value." Eisek obeyed the dream and made the long, long journey to Prague by foot. When he got there, he found the bridge, just as it had been in his dream. But to his great dismay, there were guards patrolling the bridge, so he did not dare to dig for the treasure. He stood around wondering what to do, until one of the guards, noticing him there, asked him if he had lost something. The rabbi told him about his dream. "You poor man," the guard laughed, "to have traveled all this way only because of a dream. Why I had a foolish dream like that once, and in my dream, a voice told me to go to Cracow, the capital of Poland, and there to look for the home of a devout rabbi named Eisek. And in my dream a voice told me that I would find a great treasure buried in a dirty corner behind the stove in Rabbi Eisek's house." Flabbergasted, Rabbi Eisek thanked the guard profusely and hurried back to Cracow as fast as his feet could carry him. There he dug in the corner behind the stove in his very own kitchen and found the treasure, thus putting an end to his poverty.

* * *

NOW YOU SEE GOD, NOW YOU DON'T

"O Lord...why do you hide your face from me?"
Psalm 88:14

I often use a prayer that begins with these words: "Holy God, our loving Creator, close to us as breathing and distant as the farthest star...." Those two phrases -- "close to us as breathing" and "distant as the farthest star" -- describe my experience of God. There are moments when God feels as close as my breathing. There are other times, sometimes long ones, when God seems as distant as the farthest star.

The farthest star is far indeed. Someone once figured

that if you wanted to get to the *closest* star by automobile, you would have to drive sixty miles per hour for forty-million years to get there.   There are times when God seems that remote, that inaccessible. One of the Psalmists puts it this way:

"I cry aloud to God, that he may hear me. In the day of my trouble I seek the Lord; in the night my hand is stretched out....; my soul refuses to be comforted. I think of God, and I moan...I meditate and search my spirit. Will the Lord never again be favorable? Has his steadfast love forever ceased?...Has God forgotten to be gracious? Has he in anger shut up his compassion?" (Excerpted verses from *Psalm* 77)

There it is again -- distant as the farthest star. I remind myself that even some of the greatest spirits of history have experienced God's elusiveness just as I do. If you live in a northern clime, it is helpful to know in advance that at times the weather is going to turn cold.   In much the same way, it is helpful to know that there will be spiritual seasons of bleakness in our souls. It is also helpful to know that eventually the warmth of Spring will come again.

*   *   *

WINTER IN MY HEART

One night in December, winter winds shrieked and howled outside my windows.   I felt wintry in my heart as well, fell into one of my dark places and slept poorly.

Several events had conspired to precipitate my wintry plunge. A crisis at our church had built up a full head of steam about which both my wife and I were emotionally strung-out. Also, as happens from time to time, our own relationship at home was tense as well. Feeling she had withdrawn from me, I plunged into loneliness, rejection and abandonment and couldn't shake the feelings.

I attempted to shift my state of mind by praying, only to find that God, too, seemed distant. In retrospect, I know that neither my wife nor God was so distant as I felt at the time, but my emotions overwhelmed my perspective. As I said, it was winter in my heart -- winter outside, winter inside.   Both possessed me.

I had discovered in previous wintry times that Martin

Marty's book, *A Cry of Absence*, was helpful, so I turned to him again. The words leaped out at me: ***"Winter can...blow into surprising regions of the heart when it is least expected. Such frigid assaults can overtake the spirit with the persistence of an ice age, the chronic cutting of an Arctic wind."*** Then came additional words which explained precisely what was happening in my relationship with my wife: ***"Winterly frost comes in the void left when love dies or when a lover grows distant Let a new love come into life or let the enduring one come close again, and summer can return to the heart."***

I read those words and was blessed with the feeling that *someone*, at least, knew exactly what I was feeling. Martin Marty doesn't even know I exist, but on that wintry night, and on some wintry days as well, I felt as if Martin were my friend.

In my more balanced moments, I know that in just such ways God is present to me, incarnated in some person or event. In my wintry moments, I find it helpful to remind myself who those persons have been for me in the past and then to return to them for nourishment and warmth in the present.

Who have those persons been for you?

* * *

BEYOND RATIONALITY

We must beware lest...our dogmas overthink the mystery.

Abraham Heschel
in *I Asked for Wonder*

Carl Jung, the renowned psychiatrist, believed that in order to be healthy and whole we must accept the fact that we live in a world which in many ways is mysterious. His own life persuaded him that much of what happens to us remains inexplicable. We have to know, he believed, that the unexpected and the incredible belong in this world.

Like Jung, Albert Einstein insisted that some things are simply impenetrable. He believed that to accept this fact as a reality was what it meant to have a religious attitude toward life. In this sense, at least, he considered himself devoutly religious.

Those of us who have been raised with a scientific world view often get so mesmerized by physical and material facts and by empirical approaches to reality that we lose sight of what lies beyond those facts. Our obsession with that which is provable and rationally explainable may even be one of the sources of our western malaise, not to mention our own personal yearnings for something more meaningful and satisfying to our souls. What a relief it is to simply to accept the inexplicable, to expect the unexpected, to relax with that which is impenetrable, and not only to accept mystery but also to revel in it.

*   *   *

THE FANATIC AND THE MUGWUMP

Life is full of opposing ideas with which we have to live even though we cannot resolve them -- for example, belief in God and skepticism about belief in God. That polarity gave rise to the well-known prayer, "I believe; help thou my unbelief."

Polarities are galling to people who want a clearly-defined true/false, right/wrong. One of the lessons of history is that most of us are tempted to latch on to one polarity and exclude the other. This tends to lead to extremism and fanaticism. The fanatic accepts one extreme as absolute truth and rejects the other as absolute falsehood. The relativist, on the other hand, can easily become so paralyzed by the mere existence of polarities that he cannot make up his mind to take a stand for anything.

When this happens to me, I call myself a mugwump, a mugwump being a bird that sits on the fence with its mug on one side and its wump on the other. The fanatic tends toward passionate intolerance; the mugwump tends toward tolerant indecisiveness. The first is blinded by devotion to absolutes; the second is paralyzed by insistence on relativities.

Because polarities are inevitable, I am committed to open-mindedness and tolerance of differences. Therefore, I find myself passionately intolerant of intolerance! I tend to believe there are at least two sides to almost everything. I try to operate by the principle that as soon as I have arrived at any position, I should try to find some truth in the opposite point of view as well. This makes it difficult to come down firmly anywhere. On the positive side, this approach makes for an environment that invites exploration, discussion and dialogue. On the negative side, it creates ambivalence, uncertainty, and passivity.

Those of us who lean toward mugwumpishness find ourselves all too often neutralized by our insistence on seeing many sides at once. We need to consider that in some situations that position may be as morally insidious as the fanatic's one-sidedness and intolerance.

It has been said that ambivalence is a sacred emotion. Why? Because it keeps doors open in the search for truth. It ceases to be sacred when the ambivalence paralyzes us and keeps us from decisive action.

* * *

THE TEMPTATION TO OVER-SIMPLIFY

I am increasingly impatient with complex theological discussion. I resist reading it; I resist talking about it. Perhaps this is because of some intellectual deficiency on my part. Or perhaps such discussions do not strike me as particularly relevant to most of my own questions about life and ultimate meaning. Or perhaps my impatience is because as a pastor I never found sophisticated theology much help to folks. Whatever the reason, I am prone to the temptation to simplify, perhaps even to over-simplify.

Politicians are particularly vulnerable to the temptation to over-simplification of religion, none more so, perhaps, than Dwight Eisenhower, who once remarked that people should practice their faith, "and I don't care what it is!" As my friend, Rob McCall, recently put it, "Most Americans would probably say they are of the view that it doesn't matter what your faith is as long as you practice it." To see the fallacy and the danger in this one need only be reminded that Hitler, Stalin, and Marx all had incredible faith in certain principles and practiced their faith extremely well.

The story is told about an ethicist and an astronomer who were conversing about their respective fields of expertise. "You know,"said the astronomer to the ethicist, "it seems to me that when you boil it all down, what you are saying is 'Do unto others as you would have them do unto you.'" "Well, it seems to me," replied the ethicist, "that when you boil it all down, what you are saying is 'Twinkle, twinkle little star, how I wonder what you are.'"

The desire to simplify often tempts us to *over*-simplify. However, having warned ourselves of that danger, there is still something to be said for keeping our religion simple. Fortunately, for Christians at least, Jesus was a master of

22

simplification. At the time, some of the great thinkers of the Jewish faith must have thought Jesus was *over*-simplifying when he took all the laws of the Pharisees and reduced them to two essentials: love God with heart, soul, mind and strength, and love your neighbor as yourself.

In my preference for simplification, I know that I am often guilty of *over* simplification.   Nonetheless, when all is said and done, I still prefer this to the equally dangerous temptation to over-*complicate*.   I am glad I have colleagues and friends whose intellects and dispositions enable them to confront theological complexities head-on and in depth.   I hope they, in turn, can be glad to have a colleague and friend who leans in the other direction. Perhaps we can help each other keep our balance.

* * *

THE CAPACITY TO BLUNDER SLIGHTLY

I don't like to make mistakes, but that does not prevent my making them. I comfort myself by remembering that without the historic blunderings of biological development we would probably still be anaerobic bacteria. Biologists remind us that mistakes have not only marked the path of progress but have been essential to it.

I find further validation of the value of error in William Least Heat Moon's *Blue Highways.* He describes in fascinating detail his meandering journey around the United States in his camper truck following what he calls 'blue highways' -- those secondary roads marked on the map in blue. Some of his best adventures and discoveries came as the result of taking wrong roads.

Errors have led to some of the most remarkable discoveries of science.   For example, Alexander Graham Bell, happened upon the telephone while working on a project to aid those who are hard of hearing. Thomas Edison was working on a telephone project when he discovered how to create a phonograph.   Errors, in other words, contain the potential for unexpected discoveries and experiences.

You don't have to stretch your mind very far to see the relationship between those words and the quest for religious faith. "Seek and you will find," said Jesus. Wandering and wondering are part of the search for God, and the most serious

23

blunder we can make is to give up the search because of our fear of being wrong.

* * *

ON PLAYING HARD TO GET

Four-year-old Callum and his mother were having a conversation over lunch. It went like this:

Callum: Is God everywhere?
Mother: Yes, dear.
Callum: Is God in this room?
Mother: Yes, he is.
Callum: Is he in my mug?
Mother (growing uneasy): Er - yes.
Callum (clamping his hand over his mug): GOT HIM!

Margaret Donaldson
in *Human Minds: an Exploration*

I don't know anything more about Callum than that, but I like him! I like the way he moves from the general to the particular, from the theoretical to the practical, from the ethereal to the specific. I doubt that he knew where he was going when he started that conversation, but he knew when he got there! I wish all theologizing could conclude so triumphantly.

Unwittingly, however, four-year-old Callum had put his finger on one of the most common and spiritually disastrous dangers in religion, namely, the temptation to assume that God can be captured, whether in a mug, a dogma, or a particular religion or creed. At the moment, this assumption is rampant in the world. In our own country we see it in various forms of the so-called Christian Right. Their proponents often tend to speak of God as if He were 'one of them' and claim to know exactly what God is thinking or saying. They give the impression that like Callum, they've "got Him." We see the same tendency in fundamentalist Judaism and its Islamic counterparts in other parts of the world as well.   In each case, the assumption stems from the tragically mistaken notion that anyone ever has the right to say of God, "Got Him."

God is much, much bigger than that. The very moment we think we've got a handle on God, He/She will proceed to slip out of our grasp. Where God is concerned, there is always --

always -- more than we can get hold of, which may be why to some of us it seems as if God is elusive.

I am discovering that no matter how far I travel on my own spiritual journey, I never arrive. There is *always* more to be explored and experienced. The moment I think, "Ah, *this* is what I've been searching for, I've finally got it!" -- in that very moment the certainty slips away, simply because God cannot be contained in any one experience, concept or belief.

Like four-year-old Callum, I would love to be able to clamp my hand over the mug of my spiritual experiences and say of God, "Got Him." Callum wanted to bring God down to his level and get hold of God once and for all. However, experience tells me something that Callum, at the age of four, couldn't possibly know, namely that God can never be brought down to our level nor contained in anyone's box. I think we would be closer to the truth of the matter if we were to tell Callum's story in reverse -- like this:

> Callum: Is God in this mug?
> Mother: Yes, dear.
> Callum: Is God in this room?
> Mother: Yes, dear.
> Callum: Is God in the sky?
> Mother: Yes, dear.
> Callum: Is God in the stars?
> Mother: Yes, dear.
> Callum: Is God in China and Africa and the North Pole?
> Mother: Yes, dear.
> Callum: Is God EVERYWHERE?
> Mother: Oh yes! Yes, Yes!

* * *

A DEFINITION OF FAITH

We cannot be in rapport with the reality of the divine except for rare, fugitive moments. How can those moments be saved for the long hours... when...we lose the sight and the drive?
Abraham Heschel
in *I Asked for Wonder*

Now faith is the assurance of things hoped for,
the conviction of things not seen.
The Letter to the Hebrews (11:1)

As I have indicated in previous reflections, I have had only a few vivid, personal experiences of God's presence -- experiences so clear, so strong that I had no doubt where they came from. I have had a larger number of experiences where I could see God at work in my life, though more often than not it was my interpretation of those events in retrospect that led me to that conclusion. However, the occasions have been few and far between when the immediate experience of God's presence was so strong and startling that no thought, reflection or interpretation were required

So what am I to do with the long, long intervals *between* those experiences? As a panelist on a Bill Moyers show suggested, faith is what you do between your last experience of the presence of God and the next one -- and it may be years. *That's* what faith is! Faith is trusting those experiences, remembering them, and allowing them to shape my understanding of reality. Faith also means that if those earlier experiences came without my seeking or expecting them, more such experiences may be awaiting me if I am open to them. I may yearn for them to occur, but I cannot force them to happen. All I can do is wait, trust, and keep the door -- or the window -- open to receive them.

* * *

I SURRENDER

Many years ago I faced a dilemma which, for the life of me, I could not resolve. One night, having reached a point of desperation, I went down on my knees beside my bed -- a posture not at all natural or habitual for me -- and prayed with all my heart for some guidance. What I said was simple, brief and to the point: "God," I prayed, "I don't know what to do. You take it from here." Not believing in literal voices from heaven, I didn't really think I heard one, but with utter and unexpected clarity I 'heard' the words, "I will." Those two words did not solve my problem nor tell me what to do, but I went to bed very much at peace with my indecision, and on waking the next morning, knew exactly what I needed to do.

Since then, I have faced quite a few dilemmas and have prayed many prayers. Though I have often found the praying helpful, I have never again experienced the same clarity and resolution that I did that night. I wonder at times what happened that night that made it different? On the night I have described, I was aware of a total surrendering of my will to God's will, whatever that might turn out to be. I had let go of any conscious or unconscious agenda I might have harbored. My experience was a mini-version of what was going on in the Garden of Gethsemane when Jesus prayed, *"Not my will, but thine be done." (Luke 22:42)*

My guess is that God can get through to us with such clarity only when there is total and genuine openness of mind, heart, and spirit. I know that in most of my praying I do not totally let go of my own wishes and agendas. On that particular night I did. That, I think, was the difference.

* * *

HEAD VS. HEART

All too often we assume that to have faith in God is simply to accept the *idea* that God exists. There is a far better way to look at this, namely to see faith as having to do with a *relationship*, not just an *idea*. Believing in God -- an idea in the head -- is quite a different matter, for example, than *trusting* God -- a relationship of the heart. An old story helps clarify the difference between believing in God and trusting God:

There once was a professional tight-rope walker, so the story goes, who strung a cable across Niagara Falls, and advertised far and wide that he would cross the Falls pushing a wheelbarrow. The day came, the crowd gathered. As he prepared to step onto the cable, the tight-rope walker turned to a man in the crowd and said, "Do you believe I can do it?"

"Yes, I do," said the spectator.

"I mean," said the tight-rope walker, "do you *really* believe I can do it?"

"Yes, I do," said the spectator.

"Then get in the wheelbarrow," said the tight-rope walker.

It was one thing to believe the tight-rope walker could cross the Falls safely, but quite another to trust him enough to get in the wheelbarrow. That is the difference between believing

27

in God and trusting God. One is a matter of the head; the other is a matter of the heart. Both are part of what true faith means.

* * *

SOUL TALK

The soul is like a wild animal -- tough, resilient, savvy, self-sufficient, and yet exceedingly shy. If we want to see a wild animal, the last thing we should do is go crashing through the woods, shouting for the creature to come out. But if we are willing to walk quietly into the woods and sit silently for an hour or two at the base of a tree, the creature we are waiting for may well emerge......

Parker J. Palmer
in *Let Your Life Speak*

Talking about soul has become more acceptable than it used to be. For example, there is soul food, and there is soul music. The Bible is full of soul talk: "My soul doth magnify the Lord," said Mary. "Bless the Lord, O my soul," wrote the Psalmist. When something is particularly satisfying to us, we sometimes say, "That was good for my soul."   John Baillie begins a prayer, "O God, give me grace so to live this day that whatever else I lose, I may not lose my soul."

I doubt whether we all mean the same thing when we use the word, 'soul.'   What *I* mean by soul is that deep-down core of who I am and who you are -- whom God created us to be. The question I need to ask myself over and over again is simply, 'Is it well with my soul?' In other words, am I paying adequate attention to that deep-down core of who I am and whom God intends me to be?

As I reflect on my years in ministry, it occurs to me I did not ask that question of myself or of others as often or as plainly as I could have or should have. At its best, perhaps, that's what a pastoral visit should be about -- in one way or another to ask, 'Is it well with your soul?'

I read recently about a Dr. Komp, a well-known doctor who, to my amazement, and probably the amazement of some of her patients, sometimes asks that question.   At the time I read about her, she was a professor of pediatrics at Yale School of

Medicine and former chief of a pediatric hematology/oncology department. She tells about two women, each of whom had a child with cancer. Here were two women facing the same medical crisis. Each came with her own distinct personality. Each came with a totally different way of approaching her crisis. But Dr. Komp asked both of them the identical question: 'Is it well with your soul?' Surely that was not what they expected to hear from the doctor! Oh, for more doctors who know enough to ask that question -- whatever words they choose -- and then are willing to stick around long enough to hear the answer! Oh, for more clergy who would do likewise! Oh, for more church members and friends who would find ways to ask it at the appropriate moments!

So today I am thinking about soul -- mine and yours. Is it well with my soul, I ask myself. Is it well with yours?

* * *

ATTENTION! A TENSION

Before I go to the kitchen to prepare breakfast each morning, I like to set aside an hour or so to sit in my favorite chair in my study. This is usually the most peaceful time of my day. Outside my window is an old stone wall which borders the quiet lane on which I live. The sight of it settles my spirit and "rinses my eyes," to use a phrase by May Sarton.

My study is what I call my 'China room,' with pictures on every wall that remind me of the country where I was born and which holds so many treasured childhood memories. A mobile made of small, weathered pieces of driftwood, exquisitely sensitive to even the subtlest currents of air, turns slowly and peacefully in one corner. On my desk are pictures of two of the special loves in my life -- a photo of my son taken only a year before his death, and beside it a picture of my wife, barefoot and tanned, sitting on the rocks at Acadia National Park on the coast of Maine. On a shelf near my chair is a pile of novels waiting to be read. On another shelf are some favorite books of poetry. At my elbow are the primary resources for my early morning quiet time -- a collection of devotional materials and my journal. Now is the time to lay aside my lists of things to do, my unfulfilled tasks and projects, and all the other necessities of daily living, and to draw inward, to be still, to nurture the Spirit within me. This is a time of blessed quiet, my primary way of trying to ensure that I will not quench the fire that is within me.

Unfortunately, the more I succeed in establishing harmonious, peaceful and nourishing times for withdrawal, the more resentful I become of the tasks awaiting me when I emerge. This creates tension in me. When I open my window to the world, I see and hear all the needs that call for my attention and my caring. I think, for example, of a committee of which I have somehow become the chairman. There are agendas to prepare and people to call about the program we are planning. There is the political campaign I am involved in to support a candidate for Governor of the State of New Hampshire. There are people to call, letters to write, envelopes to be addressed and meetings to organize. There is a young friend whose wife has just died of cancer and with whom I need to be in touch. There is my little grandson, Noah, with cerebral palsy and his parents who are nearly overwhelmed by all the care he needs. And there is my daily 'To Do' list, which even in these retirement years is almost never completed at the end of a day. If there is something deep within that pulls me inward, there is also something deep within that pulls me outward. Always, inevitably, there is this tension.

For a contemplative person, the temptation is to retreat into quietness, to withdraw completely from the demands of the world. For an activist the temptation is to plunge into the fray with total commitment, neglecting the inner life. The trick is to find a way to keep a balance between the two opposing poles.

Rabbi Abraham Heschel -- writer, theologian, spiritual giant -- successfully combined both poles. When he died, there were two books beside his bed. One was a Hasidic classic, the other a book on the war in Vietnam. In an anthology of Heschel's writings, Samuel Dresner suggests that these two books are symbolic of the polarities with which Heschel lived -- mystic and social activist, deeply committed both to the eternal spirit and the mundane here-and-now, choosing neither over the other, accepting the tension between them.

Like Heschel, most of the great 'Spirit People' of the ages have found a way to do this. Jesus, for example, frequently withdrew into the desert to pray, to reflect and to reconnect with the Source of his strength. From time to time, in order to keep his balance, he literally walked away from crying needs . There must have been people who felt abandoned when he did this. They needed him *now*. He must have been tempted to stay, for the needs were endless. But he *knew* he needed to keep a balance between the inner and the outer.

I expected that in retirement it would be easy to achieve that balance, but even now, when I can exercise considerable control over my schedule, balance is hard to maintain. The tension between inner and outer remains a fact of life. I have learned, however, that when I allow myself to get stuck too long in one polarity to the neglect of the other, my conscience -- or perhaps it is the Holy Spirit -- can be counted on to get my attention and pull me back to the other. In the long run, things seem to balance fairly well. In the short run, they will probably always feel out of balance. When that happens, there is inevitably a tension that gets my attention and pulls me back the other way. Not a bad arrangement, when all is said and done.

* * *

BE STILL AND KNOW

To pray does not mean to listen to oneself speaking. Prayer involves becoming silent, and being silent, and being silent, and waiting until God is heard.
Soren Kierkegaard

For God alone my soul waits in silence.
Psalm 62:1

Be still, and know that I am God!
Psalm 46:10

One Wednesday noon I met with a group of local clergy at the rectory of the Catholic Church in Concord, Massachusetts. On this beautiful warm June day, the priest gathered us on a screened porch on the south side of the rectory. The breeze was refreshing, and my eye could take in the center of the town from a perspective I had never seen before. We exclaimed at the beauty and peacefulness of the porch. Thinking how pleasant it would be to work in a spot like that, I said to the priest, "I think this would be a great place to put your desk!" My Episcopalian colleague responded immediately. "Tuck, your Puritan heritage is showing!" gently chiding me for wishing to bring my work into a place of such rest, beauty and peace. I protested, arguing that if you have to work you might as well do it in as beautiful a place as possible. But my colleague had a point. This lovely place was made-to-order for *escape,* a place to get *away* from work.

Places of quiet escape are a spiritual necessity. Jesus found quiet by escaping to the desert, Elijah by holing up in a remote cave. As for me, I retreat to my study at home. Because I am retired, I no longer have to go to work every morning and meet constant deadlines. However, I have learned that finding places where I can have quiet is still an urgent need.

This is a basic rule of the Soul -- first you must have the quiet. This need is so basic that the ancient Hebrews considered a day of rest to be one of the Ten Commandments.

Barrie Shepherd writes about the importance of being still:

> *I read a curious tale recently*
> *about an ancient, dusty city in the land of Israel*
> *in which, so they say, there are pure underground*
> *rivers of water that rush beneath the busy streets.*
> *But it is only after dark, in the stillness,*
> *when those streets are all deserted, that one can*
> *hear their gurgling sounds, and realize*
> *that they are really there.*
>
> in *Praying the Psalms*

I find it hardest to be aware of the presence of God when I am busy, when the sounds that drift in my window are noisiest and most insistent. I wish this were not so, but the clutter and clatter of life gets in my way, and I need to find ways each day to be still -- not that God is absent, only that when the externals intrude too clamorously I lose what little conscious contact I have with God.

How we achieve stillness is an individual matter. We will differ in the times and places we choose. For me, an hour, or even just a half hour before breakfast each day works best. When I drift away from this too many days in a row, I pay a price. I become less calm, less centered, more irritable, disjointed and ill at ease. In Tennyson's words, stillness is what makes it possible to "hear a deeper voice above the storm." Be still.

* * *

MEDITATING ON THE RUN

Cardiovascular experts and skilled meditators recommend that in order to get the most out of our exercise or our meditation we stick with it for a minimum of twenty minutes. Say what you will about the virtues and benefits of twenty-minute meditations, the fact remains that many people simply will not take that much time.

Is there an alternative? Probably not, at least nothing that will provide the same quality of experience. However, whether we meditate for relatively long periods of time or count ourselves among those who simply cannot or will not slow down long enough to do so, there are some other approaches.

For example, I recently heard Dr. David Treadway, a well-known psychotherapist and popular author, give a lecture in which he suggested that each of us can enrich our lives by doing three one-minute meditations each day.

1) In the first hour of each day, designate one minute
       to be quiet.

2) In the second hour of each day, designate one minute
       to meditate

3) In the third hour of each day, take one minute
       to pray.

When he finished his lecture, someone in the audience rose to suggest that we designate a fourth hour of each day to say thank you.

Four minutes a day! To a person who is serious about developing a deeper prayer life or becoming a meditator, these four one-minute pauses may not be much. But short pauses have the virtue of being eminently do-able and are a great deal better than ignoring the inner life completely.

Whether I meditate for long periods of each day or not, I find it useful at the end of each day, to ask myself two questions:

1) **For what moments in this day am I least grateful?** What in this day felt fragmented, ragged, rough-edged, incomplete? What drained me? What left me feeling diminished? Then having named these moments, I remind myself of the Bible verse, *"Cast all your anxieties on God, for God cares about you."* *(I Peter 5:7)*

2) **For what moments in this day am I most grateful?** During my waking hours, what made life feel whole, worthwhile and satisfying? What were the moments of beauty and love? What left me feeling fulfilled -- or filled full? Then I remind myself of the Bible verse, *"Whatever is true, whatever is honorable, whatever is just, whatever is pure,,, if there is any*

excellence and if there is anything worthy of praise, think about these things." (*Philippians* 4:8)

These two questions pull together the loose ends of my day. I find it a good way to end the day and conducive to a restful night.

* * *

CREATIVE DROUGHT

There are days, sometimes even weeks or months, when the creative juices simply refuse to flow. I sit down to write, but nothing comes. I am comforted by the knowledge that most writers go through times of dryness.

Doris Grumbach claims that the phrase, 'creative drought,' is an oxymoron, by which she means that the two words are contradictory. I disagree. There really *is* such a thing as a drought which is creative -- times when the drought itself is the prerequisite for creativity and should be seen as part and parcel of the creative process.

Drought, of course, is a non-productive time. Nevertheless, out of non-productivity, dryness, and emptiness may come the impetus to step back from activity and become more reflective. For me, times of drought often serve as the 'ants in the pants' which lead to renewed creativity and a more intentional regrouping of my mind, body and heart.

We are told that Jesus, like many other great Spirit People of the ages, retreated to the desert to replenish himself. He deliberately sought out a dry place in order to counter his own dryness. He went to a place of drought in order to be filled. Jesus did this intentionally, but I find that more often than not such times are forced upon me by mood and circumstance. Either way, those periods of drought and dryness serve to remind me that the wells of my spirit need to be replenished, thus becoming the impetus for me to do something about this condition.. In other words, the vacuum invites me to do whatever I can in order to be filled.

For this reason, neither we nor nature should abhor a vacuum.

* * *

PRAYER AS "TAKING COUNSEL"

Prayer is not a way to tell God how I would run the world if I were God. Nor is it is a way to give God all the up-to-the-minute information that I think God ought to have. Rather, prayer is consulting God to help me figure out how God might live if God were in *my* place. Abraham Heschel calls it *"taking counsel with what we know about the will of God."* He also describes prayer as dreaming *"in league with God."*

There is no special mystery about "taking counsel" with what we already know about the will of God. The truth is we *do* know some things about the will of God -- or at least we have some powerful clues. That's an important part of what Jesus does for us -- he makes visible the invisible. This is what the great spiritual figures of history and the great spiritual writings are all about -- making visible the invisible. Good praying is therefore contingent, in one sense, on our being familiar with what the great minds and spirits of history have discerned. Otherwise, we pray in something of a moral and spiritual vacuum. So prayer, at least in part, is a deliberate act of consulting what we already know, checking it out, weighing our current need or decision in the light of what we already know about God. For me, at least, that changes my perspective, sometimes quite dramatically.

If prayer were nothing more than that, it would still be crucial for wise decision-making.

* * *

COLOR MY EARS RED

Judas is only the first in a procession of betrayers two thousand years long. If Jesus were to exclude him from his love and forgiveness, to one degree or another he would have to exclude mankind.
Frederick Buechner
in *The Faces of Jesus*

At the Last Supper Jesus predicted that one of the disciples would betray him. They all asked, "Lord, is it I?" In a mosaic which portrays this story, the ears of all the disciples are red, but Judas' ears are a little redder!

Traditionally, Judas has been portrayed as a betrayer, the

bad guy, the villain of the story, the one whose ears are appropriately redder than all the others. But the truth is that I have a lot in common with Judas, as do most of us. There is no way I can self-righteously claim to be a faithful follower of Jesus. In many ways, I am not only less than faithful, but am actually *un*faithful, which is to confess that I do some things I ought not to do, and do not do some things I ought to do.

Parishioners have often told me they feel they cannot take Communion because they aren't 'good enough.' The point of the mosaic described above, it seems to me, is that *none* of us is 'good enough.' We *all* have red ears.

Dr. Andrew Canale, a Roman Catholic psychologist, suggests that the true spirit of Jesus and of Christianity at its best is expressed by the priest who faces the congregation, lifts up the Host, and says, ***"Those of you who feel unworthy to come to communion, know that communion is for you especially. Come."*** *Especially* it is for those of us whose ears are reddest.

O God, you know me as I am. You know that I am both for you and against you. I have some of the noblest of yearnings and some of the basest of yearnings. I know the heights of love and the depths of self-centeredness. For the unspeakable gift of my highest and best possibilities, I thank you from the bottom of my heart. And for my unspeakable failures of love and compassion, I most humbly ask your forgiveness. Forgive my sins, those I know, those I dare not name, and those of which I am not even aware. By your grace accept me as I am and make of me more than I can imagine. Amen

* * *

I CONFESS

Many of my parishioners were turned off by public prayers of confession. One Sunday, upset by one of those prayers, a worshiper counted up the number of sins he found included in a prayer I had printed in the worship bulletin, complained the list was much too long and claimed he had never committed a single one of them. For me it was just the opposite -- I thought it a rather short list and felt I had committed all of them!

Unlike those who resist such prayers, I find it very helpful from time to time to name the ways in which I have

missed the mark. Here are a few of them, all of which I have seen in various printed prayers so that I know I am not alone in experiencing them:
- a fretful disposition
- a reluctance to bear the burdens of others
- an undue willingness to let others bear *my* burdens
- fine words, shabby thoughts
- friendly face, cool heart
- much love and beauty unappreciated, and many
  blessings unacknowledged or taken for granted
- needless anxieties and fruitless fears
- failure to be true even to my own accepted standards

Not one of the above "sins" describes *all* of what I am, of course, nor do most of them persist in me all the time. And of course the list is not complete. I could make a longer one.

What would *your* list look like? And having made that list, do you also remind yourself of God's promise of forgiveness? No prayer of confession is complete until that assurance of forgiveness is also taken to heart.

* * *

ON BEING RELIGIOUS WITHOUT SOUNDING THAT WAY

Barbara Brown Taylor says of Garrison Keillor that ***"Without using one theological word, he managed to illumine the holiness of common life on earth."*** That is one of the reasons I like Keillor. People who can speak of deeply religious matters without using traditional religious language delight my soul.   Some of my favorite authors are writers who excel in this art --   Annie Dillard, Loren Eiseley, Henry David Thoreau, Robert Fulghum and E.B. White, for example. Though most of them would probably be amazed to be included, I consider them allies in ministry. They touch my soul without using 'God-talk.'

For example, one of E.B.White's grandchildren was born during the Christmas season. Here is how he described that particular nativity:

Instead of following a star, we simply followed directions given us by the child's parents; took the ten o'clock train, and found the infant in Boston, where it lay behind glass in a hospital.   No shepherds were abiding there, but there was a nurse in a mask attending, and the glory of the Lord shone round about -- a child seen through a glass clearly.

Elledge Scott
in *E.B.White: a Biography*

There is nothing pious here about the holy quality of a child's birth -- just a simple reminder, couched in some light humor, of what a sacred moment this is.

Henry David Thoreau was one of White's philosophical and literary heroes. Deeply impressed by Henry David Thoreau's ability to write about spiritual matters without sounding religious White writes that Thoreau's *Walden*

"...is like an invitation to life's dance, assuring the troubled recipient that no matter what befalls him in the way of success or failure, he will always be welcome at the party -- that the music is played for him, too, if he will listen and move his feet....it contains religious feeling without religious images, and it steadfastly refuses to record bad news."

Elledge Scott
in *E.B.White: a Biography*

Now if that isn't a religious statement, what *is*? What better way to describe the Good News than the reminder that you are "always welcome at the party," and that "the music is played for you too," and all you have to do is listen and move your feet? Here are no ought's, no should's, no have-to's -- just an invitation and a welcome, no matter who, no matter what. All we have to do is come.

* * *

MOUNTAIN DAY

It is a tradition at the Northfield/Mt. Hermon Schools that on some crisp, clear Autumn day someone in charge declares it to be Mountain Day. Classes and other activities are canceled, and off everyone goes to climb a mountain together. It's a good tradition. We all should take a 'mountain day' from time to time, even if we no longer can climb mountains.

Once upon a time, the Bible tells us, Jesus declared a mountain day. He took three friends along -- just the three, nobody else, and took a hike up a high mountain, a place apart. This was no Mt. Monadnock, or Mt. Chocorua, or Mt. Fujiyama where almost any fine day you are likely to meet a crowd on the summit or along the trail. It wasn't that kind of mountain. There were just the four of them -- Jesus, Peter, James and John -- alone.

We are told that up there on the mountain, right there before their eyes, Jesus was 'transfigured.' In Christian tradition this is considered an important event. There is even a day designated as Transfiguration Sunday. Raphael went to great lengths to paint the event as he imagined it. Jesus, dressed in dazzling white, is wearing a somewhat sickly, ethereal smile. Floating about three feet in the air, his eyes rolled up toward heaven, he appears not to be well-grounded. In awe or terror or both, his three hiking buddies are cowering below him. Two of them are literally hiding their faces; the other risks a tentative peek.

I've never liked this story. I cannot recall ever having preached about it. Raphael's attempt to capture it on canvas doesn't help me a bit. His portrayal is too other-worldly, too far removed from my experience and imagination.

Now, suddenly, it dawns on me what this may be about. What if the point of this story is not what happened to Jesus but what happened to the disciples? What if *they* were the ones who were transformed? Suppose this is about their ability, at last, to see Jesus as he really was? What if this is about what Marcus Borg calls "meeting Jesus again for the first time?"

Sometimes I would like something like that to happen to me -- to see Jesus as if for the first time, my eyes unclouded by years of accumulated assumptions and over-familiarity. I've grown accustomed to his face. He's become old hat. I feel fettered by the encrustations of the familiar. But the experience *could* happen to me just as it does from time to time with an old friend or someone I love -- suddenly a flash of recognition of who she is, who she really is and has been all the time, seen now through new eyes, sometimes only for a moment. For that moment, at least, he/she is transfigured. It *could* happen, I suppose, with Jesus. But first I might need to take a long hard hike with him, take the time, make the effort, sweat a bit. I think the fact that it happened to Peter, James and John on a *high* mountain, a place apart, all alone was no accident.

Maybe that's why only three of the disciples went along that day. Maybe Jesus said, "Let's call it a mountain day," and only three of them took him up on it. The rest of them -- like me -- weren't ready to take the time and make the climb.

* * *

DON'T TRY TO TAME A WILD MAN

It was mid-January. Christmas trees had been removed and the decorations carefully stored in their boxes until next year. Adults had put Christmas behind them.   But for my five-year-old grandson, David, Christmas was still very much in the air. The carols lingered in his heart, and he sang them as if Christmas were still happening. His mother listened with less than half an ear, for the season had passed and one can grow tired of even such loveliness as Christmas carols. But as he sang, it gradually dawned on her that he was singing a familiar carol with a fresh twist. Here is how it went:

> *Silent night, holy night, all is calm, all is bright,*
> *Round yon virgin, mother and child,*
> *Holy infant, so tender and WILD...*

I *like* David's version! Tender and *wild* seems a whole lot closer to the truth about Jesus than tender and *mild*. Mild, after all, according to my dictionary, suggests moderate, temperate, not extreme in any way. Tell that to the Pharisees! Tell it to the disciples whose encounter with Jesus turned them upside down, and in some cases cost them their lives.

But *wild*? Is that really the right word? Sometimes we can get at the meaning of a word by exploring its opposite. So, what's the opposite of wild? Tame comes to mind. We tame wild animals. A barnyard goose is a tamed, domesticated version of a wild goose. The opposite of Jesus as a wild man would be Jesus as a tame man. Tame, according to the dictionary, suggests such things as :

- easy to control
- submissive
- dull
- without spirit or force

That's not Jesus! No way. Wild, on the other hand, suggests

-exciting
-spirited

40

-fresh
-free
-unfettered
-virile
-startling

So, young David, I think you got it right! Keep singing it *your* way. And when next Christmas comes around, I'll sing it your way, too!

*   *   *

ONCE UPON A TIME

There must be thousands of ways of telling the Christmas story -- shepherds, wise men, angels, Tiny Tim, Scrooge, a star in the East, even Santa Claus. Each attempts in its own way to capture and convey something of the mystery and excitement of what Christians have called the Incarnation. For me, however, few stories capture Christmas as well as the one I am about to tell you. It goes like this:

She was five,
sure of the facts,
and recited them
with slow solemnity,
convinced every word
was revelation.

She said they were so poor they had only
peanut butter and jelly sandwiches to
eat, and they went a long way from
home without getting lost. The lady
rode a donkey, the man walked, and
the baby was inside the lady.
They had to stay in a stable with an ox
and an ass (hee-hee), but the Three
Rich Men found them because a star
lited the roof.
Shepherds came, and you could pet the sheep
but not feed them.

Then the baby was borned.

And do you know who he was?
          Her quarter eyes inflated
          to silver dollars.

The baby was God!
          And she jumped in the air,
          whirled round, dove into the sofa,
          and buried her head under the
          cushion
          which is the only proper response to
          the Good News of the Incarnation.
                    John Shea
                    in *The Hour of the Unexpected*
There you have it!

* * *

LEARNING TO FLY

What many people are looking for when they go to church is comfort. That may not be all they want, but it's one of the primary things they want. Life, after all, is hard. Life is demanding. Life is hurried. Therefore, it is natural to want a place where we can go from time to time that will soothe us, calm us, relax us, make us feel good, or at least make us feel better. I want that, too -- for them and for myself.

But church is not always like that. Sometimes instead of comforting us, it challenges us and prods us toward some change of thinking, believing, acting. Sometimes, in fact, going to church is downright uncomfortable. It *ought* to be!

It is helpful to reflect on the fact that in nature, good mothering is sometimes very demanding and tough. A mother bird knows, for example, that at some point she must push her young out into the world. If she thought it a priority to protect her young, soothe them, calm them, relax them, and make them comfortable, they would never learn to fly. So what does she do? She *pushes* them!

          Come to the edge;
                    we might fall.
          Come to the edge;
                    it's too high.
          COME TO THE EDGE;

42

And they came,
And she pushed them...
And they flew.

Apollinaire

I once had a dream about a young man who was very shy, retiring, humble and withdrawn, and who concluded that therefore he was very Christ-like. In my dream, I strongly disagreed with him. I thought he was much too passive, soft, bland, unexciting and ineffective to be Christ-like. So, with passion in my voice, I gave him some advice. I said to this soft, passive, humble young man, "Christ, you old devil, go out and steal the show!" I wanted to shake him up, challenge him, push him out of his comfortable nest and force him to fly. I wanted to see some pizzazz, some excitement, some cutting edge.

It doesn't take a dream-expert to suspect that this advice was addressed to myself, not to the church. But the message has an implication for the church as well. I believe that any church worth its salt will, on occasion, choose not to comfort its worshipers, but to challenge them to "go out and steal the show."

The next time I go to church and am pushed to approach 'the edge,' I want to remind myself that the moment I feel most uncomfortable may be the very one when I could learn to fly!

* * *

HARVEST AND GRACE

Last night, little goblins came Halloweening at our door. In order to get here, they had shuffled noisily through piles of dried leaves in our driveway. This morning, there is a nip in the air and frost on the pumpkin by the lamppost in our front yard. We have put the garden to bed. Thanksgiving is just around the corner, and we have been on the telephone making plans for a family gathering.

In *A Timbered Choir,* Wendell Berry reminds me what this time of year is all about.

Harvest will fill the barn; for that
The hand must ache, the face must sweat.
And yet no leaf or grain is filled
By work of ours; the field is tilled

43

And left to grace. That we may reap,
Great work is done while we're asleep.

I hear a refreshing note of humility in that poem. "*...no* leaf or grain is filled by work of ours; the field is tilled and left to grace....Great work is done while we're asleep." In short, it's not all up to us. We easily forget that whatever success we may experience, whatever accomplishments are ours, is due in large part to grace at work behind the scenes -- even while we sleep. Think with me, then, about grace for a moment.
- Grace resides in all those who have aided and supported us along the way.
- Grace resides in all the circumstances beyond our control which contribute to the fulfilling of our tasks.
- Grace resides in the genetic gifts we inherited -- gifts of strength and will, intelligence and creativity.
- Grace resides in the gift of sleep -- the necessary period of rest for renewal of mind, body, perspective and imagination.
- Grace resides in the flash of insight that comes to us in the middle of the night and solves the problem that stymied us while wide awake.
- Grace resides in the dreams that heal and sometimes guide us.

All of this is grace. That's what thanksgiving -- or Thanksgiving -- is all really about.

I propose an assignment, namely, that you make your own list of the graces in your life. When you have created your list, you will be ready for Thanksgiving -- not only on the last Thursday in November, but any day of the year.

* * *

A BLESSING FOR THE WORLD

At the conclusion of a Kirkridge retreat called, 'Ministering to the Soul of the Nation,' I stood with seventy-five men and women in a lodge at the top of a mountain in the Poconos. We had spent several days together, and now, as a final act, had just celebrated Communion. A Roman Catholic priest had been invited to give the final blessing. He asked us to turn and face outward through the wide bank of tall windows.

44

The hills and valleys of our precious nation and planet spread out before us reminding us of our intimate connectedness and interdependence with all of nature, with all humanity. ***"God has made of one blood all the nations of the earth,"*** he said. Then he asked us all to raise our hands in blessing and benediction over that precious world. As I did so, along with all the others, tears began to stream down my face as my heart welled up with the love and the pain I felt for the world.

The priest then reminded us that as Christians our first names were given to us -- Tom, Dick, Mary, Tuck, Susan. But our last name, he said, the name carried by each of us, is Christ. We are called, he continued, to 'be Christs' to each other, to the nation, and to the planet earth.

We sang a hymn, then we went out and returned home to be 'Christs' wherever we lived -- imperfect, flawed human beings, to do the best we could wherever we could.

* * *

II. ON BEING MORE FULLY ALIVE

"For man, the vast marvel is to be alive....We ought to dance with rapture that we should be alive and in the flesh, and part of the living, incarnate cosmos."
David Herbert Lawrence

WAKE UP!

Introducing Part II

"Only that day dawns to which we are awake."
Henry David Thoreau
Walden

Some readers might assume that by the time one has reached his mid-seventies, as I have, he should be about as alive as he will ever get. However, it is my experience that for much of my life I have been too busy or too full of other concerns to appreciate fully what a banquet has been spread out before me. So, now, in my third-third of life, I find I am taking in more than I ever have before. I know now that there is always -- always -- far more to life than what meets the eye. Like an iceberg, there is always far more below the surface than above. To be more fully alive is to become more and more aware that this is so.

> *Let me respectfully remind you --*
> *Life and death are of supreme importance,*
> *Time swiftly passes by, and the opportunity is lost.*
> *Each of us should strive to awaken, AWAKEN.*
> *Take heed, do not squander your life.*

These words are often spoken at Zen retreats, at the end of a day -- an enticing invitation to experience life more fully. For me, this might mean waking up to the banquet of creation that lies before me in every moment. It might mean exploring a relationship more deeply, or imagining myself into a news headline about a disaster or tragic event. Waking up might mean working with a poem not yet fully understood, or paying attention to my relationship with God, or allowing myself to feel the pain, burden or grief of a friend's sickness or loss of a loved one.

One of the most awake people I know is Henry David Thoreau. He claimed that his profession was *"always to be alert...to know God's lurking places, to attend all the oratorios and the operas in nature."* That's part of what it might mean to be awake.

Here is another illustration of what the world might look like to a person who is fully awake:

> *The Creator God is a gracious, an abundant, and a*
> *generous host/hostess. She has spread out for our*

delight a banquet that was twenty billion years in the making. A banquet of rivers and lakes, of rain and sunshine, of rich earth and amazing flowers, of handsome trees and of dancing fishes, of contemplative animals and of whistling winds, of dry and wet seasons, of cold and hot climates. But it is a banquet that works, this banquet we call creation....It works for our benefit if we behave toward it as reverent guests.

Matthew Fox
in *Original Blessing*

The next few reflections are about waking up, discovering the music that makes you -- or me -- want to join the dance and then sit down to feast at the banquet, whether we are fifteen or one hundred, or somewhere in between.

* * *

A MORE DELICATE TASTE FOR JOY

...all of creation is a song of praise to God.
Hildegarde of Bingen

How sublime to look down into the workshop of nature to see her clouds, hail, snow, rain, thunder all fabricated at our feet.
Thomas Jefferson

Frederick Nietzsche was not one of history's happier philosophers. Like most of us, he was well-acquainted with the abysses of life. He writes that it is *"Out of such abysses that one returns newborn, having shed one's skin, more ticklish and malicious, with a more delicate taste for joy, with a more tender tongue for all good things, with merrier senses, with a second dangerous innocence in joy, more child-like, and yet a hundred times subtler than one has ever had before."*
That's what I would like for myself, also -- to be more 'ticklish,' to have a more tender tongue, merrier senses and a more childlike innocence in joy. I would like to develop a more delicate taste for joy.
Each of us discovers our own ways to help that happen. Photography has been one of mine. With a camera in my hand, I

50

pay closer attention to colors, shapes, patterns, light, and beauty. Even more helpful to me than photography are writers whose eyes, imaginations, knowledge, and poetic skills bring things to life in ways that open up the world for me. One of my favorites is Annie Dillard. For example, in *Pilgrim at Tinker Creek*, she writes, *"There is always an enormous temptation in all of life to diddle around making itsy-bitsy friends and meals and journeys for itsy-bitsy years on end."* She continues, *"The world is wilder than that in all directions, more dangerous and bitter, more extravagant and bright. We are making hay when we should be making whoopee; we are raising tomatoes when we should be raising Cain, or Lazarus."*

Annie Dillard lifts me out of my daily-ness and ordinariness. She invites me out of my routine, escorts me beyond that which is dull and expected. For her, it is *"as though I stand at the foot of an infinitely high staircase, down which some exuberant spirit is flinging tennis ball after tennis ball, eternally, and the one thing I want in the world is a tennis ball."* In case I still haven't got the message, she writes, *"...the extravagant gesture is the very stuff of creation. After the one extravagant gesture of creation in the first place, the universe has continued to deal exclusively in extravagances, flinging intricacies and colossi down aeons of emptiness, heaping profusions and profligacies with ever fresh vigor. The whole show has been on fire from the word go!"*

I rely on folks like Annie Dillard to wake me up to what is around me and within me. I know that if I am going to develop a more delicate taste for joy, if I am going to learn to see that the whole show has been on fire from the word go, it will be in large part because I know where I can go to get the help I need. No doubt you have your own special wake-up callers. Pay attention to them!

* * *

THE SOUND OF MUSIC

To ears that are expanded, what a harp this world is!
Henry David Thoreau

I once knew a man who was converted to Christianity by a performance of Handel's *Messiah*. Happening to him out of the blue, or so it seemed, this experience changed the direction of his entire life. My guess is that he was not the first to be so deeply affected by music, nor will he be the last. What changed him was not a preacher, not reading the Bible, not prayer, not an altar call, not a theological argument, not a life crisis. It was music.

I have no special gift for creating music, nor even much of an ear for learning it. Nevertheless, at one time or another music has tapped into almost every emotion I have ever experienced. For example:

The music from *Riverdance* excites me and makes my
heart beat faster.
The theme from *Chariots of Fire* fills me with nostalgia
because when I was a little boy I knew and idolized
Eric Little, the main character, and first heard the music
from the movie shortly after our son died.
William Boyce's *Symphonies* make me feel happy and
light in spirit.
September, especially as sung by Willie Nelson, stirs me
romantically.
Bobbie McFerrin singing *Don't Worry, Be Happy,*
brings a smile.
The second movement of Dvorak's *New World*
Symphony often chokes me up and brings tears to
my eyes. Commonly known as 'Going Home,' I
first heard it as a homesick adolescent, and even
after sixty years, this music is deeply poignant to me.
O Beautiful for Spacious Skies stirs feelings of
patriotism.
Hymns like *Immortal, Invisible, God Only Wise* and *Be*
Thou My Vision help me sense and feel the
presence of God.

When he was in the last months of his life, our son, Mark, stopped playing music on his stereo. When I asked him why, he said, "It makes me want to cry." For the same reason, after he died, I too stopped listening to music. Music often surfaced my pain at times when I couldn't stand having it

52

surfaced. There were other times, however, when I became aware that I was bottling up feelings and couldn't find a way to release them. At times like that, I would deliberately play music I knew would unlock my feelings and release tears that needed to come.

What's my point? Maybe nothing more than simply to recognize how central and powerful music is in life. From the primitive jungle drum to the Grateful Dead, to Handel, Haydn, Mozart and Rutter, music is one of God's most precious gifts.

Pat Conroy is right: *"...without music, life is a journey through a desert that has not ever heard the rumor of God."*

* * *

NEXT TIME, MAYBE....

Albert Bartholomew Thorwaldsen, a Danish sculptor, produced a total of eighty statues and one hundred and thirty-nine busts. When a friend asked him, "Which of all your statues do you consider to be your best?" Thorwaldsen replied, "The next one."

When I first read that story, I thought to myself, now *there* was a man with an eye to the future. This was a man who was not addicted to his past performances, no matter how good they may have been. He was looking ahead. He was convinced something better could yet be done. A good, healthy way of looking at life, I thought.

Or is it? I recall how all through my growing years if I came home with a C on my report card, my father would suggest that *next* time, perhaps, I could get a B. If I came home with a B, *next* time, perhaps, I could get an A. No matter how well I did, *next* time, perhaps, like Mr. Thorwaldsen, I could do better.

There was some merit in this. The challenge pushed me always to do better if I could. However, it also had the effect of making it very difficult, if not impossible, to enjoy and savor what I had already accomplished. Mr. Thorwaldsen and my father had a point, but it may also be the part of wisdom to know that doing better the *next* time is not the ultimate measure of success. Much may be said for savoring our accomplishments at each step along the way.

* * *

LOOK AROUND -- SLOWLY

On a summer day in Deerfield, Massachusetts, I visited a crafts fair. Ambling from booth to booth, I was captivated by an exhibit of photographs. One photograph in particular caught my eye, a stereotypical Vermont farm scene, spectacular mainly in its unusual and dramatic lighting. My interest in photography emboldened me to approach the man tending the booth.

"Are you the photographer?"

"I am."

"Well, I'm curious about how you got that picture. Did you spot that scene and then sit there for hours waiting for the light to change?"

"No. I can't stand waiting around for things to happen."

"So, the secret, then," I asked, "is simply to *be* there at the right moment?"

"No," he replied, "the secret is to *know* that you're there."

In somewhat similar fashion, when Moses saw the burning bush, at first he didn't see God in it. According to the Old Testament story, it was not until he "turned aside" that he heard God speaking to him. In other words, first he had to notice; then he had to stop and pay attention. Only then could he recognize God's presence in that place. Then, when Jacob spent that famous night at Bethel where he dreamed of angels on a ladder, when morning came he said to himself, ***"Surely the Lord is in this place -- and I didn't know it."*** In each case, something beautiful and profound was going on around them, and they simply didn't recognize it.

I go through much of my life that way, simply not noticing. I do not turn aside. I do not stop to take it in. Abba Besarion, a 4th century monk, said about the attentiveness required in a life of faith, ***"The monk should be all eye."*** That is surely the secret of good photography, good poetry, good almost anything at all, including spirituality.

The first criterion for experiencing God in this world is to look around - slowly. When we do, we may see all kinds of things we never saw before.

It must have been some such experience that inspired Walt Whitman to write these immortal words:

Why should I wish to see God better than this day?
I see something of God in each hour of the
twenty-four, and each moment, then,
In the faces of man and woman I see God....

54

I find letters from God dropt in the street,
and every one is signed by God's name....

If I look around -- slowly -- I might see God better every day.

* * *

THE ART OF SEEING

Look on the glories of God, and awaken to
the glory in thee.
　　　　　Jehuda Halevi
　　　　　A medieval Jewish poet

Last Saturday I went on a field trip with my photography class. Three days later, we all came back together and looked at each other's pictures. We had spent two hours at the same place, but our pictures were completely different. Though most of us had been attracted to the same subject matter, we had all seen different things and from different perspectives. Most startling of all were the pictures taken by our instructor, a professional. He had seen things none of the rest of us had seen. His technique, of course, was also better. But the major difference was in his eyes. He saw possibilities the rest of us hadn't noticed. He had what artists like to call a good eye.

When I show some of my photographs to friends, especially if they are favorably impressed, the first question they usually ask is, "What kind of camera do you use?" The assumption seems to be that if a picture is a good one, the camera must be responsible. I am learning that the most important equipment cannot be purchased at a camera store. A good picture begins with a good eye. That, not the camera, is the most important piece of equipment. Other ingredients include, for example, the quality of the film, the lens and the quality of the developing and printing. However, the art of seeing is even more important than all the equipment and technology. Seeing involves not only your eyes, but your heart, your mind, your intuition, your emotions. It requires what some people call "relaxed attentiveness."

The prophet Isaiah, who obviously never even dreamed of a camera, once wrote that a time was coming when darkness would cover the earth, but God would come and be like a light.

55

And then he wrote words which could just as well have been written in a manual on photography: *"Lift up your eyes and look around! Then you shall see...."* (60:1-5) You do that, say professional photographers, by learning how to achieve relaxed attentiveness, clearing the mind, learning how to switch yourself off and let yourself go. For me, at least, that's not quite so easy as it may sound, but the counsel is on target, both for photography and for the life that is fully awake.

* * *

I WONDER AS I WANDER

I did not ask for success; I asked for wonder. And You gave it to me."
Abraham Heschel
in I Asked for Wonder

I have a friend in his mid-seventies who, when asked what he is doing with his life answered, "I wonder a lot." At first I assumed he was referring to a sense of awe, but he tells me he meant it more in terms of questioning what life is really all about. I do that kind of wondering too. However, what I am writing about now is the kind of wonder that leads to amazement and awe, perhaps even to reverence -- the kind of wondering that Abraham Heschel is describing when he says that *"Awe...enables us to perceive in the world intimations of the divine...., to sense the ultimate in the common and the simple; to feel in the rush of passing the stillness of the eternal."* This kind of wondering is enhanced for me by a passage from John Steinbeck's *East of Eden:*

> *Sometimes a kind of glory lights up the mind of a man. It happens to nearly everyone....It is a feeling in the stomach, a delight of the nerves....The skin tastes the air, and every deep-drawn breath is sweet....It flashes in the brain and the whole world glows outside your eyes. A man may have lived all his life in the gray...dark and somber. The events, even the important ones, may have trooped by faceless and pale. And then -- the glory -- so that a cricket song sweetens his ears, the smell of the earth rises chanting to his nose, and dappling light*

under a tree blesses his eyes. Then a man pours outward, a torrent of him, and yet he is not diminished. And I guess a man's importance in the world can be measured by the quality and number of his glories....

The quality and number of our glories! Now *that* is something to wonder about!

* * *

A THANKSGIVING MYTH

There is a Thanksgiving myth which needs to be dispelled. The myth is that what we celebrate on Thanksgiving Day is abundance, good fortune, success, security and a good life. If we study the Presidential Proclamations over the years, we find the note of self-congratulation rings through many of them. They remind us of our warm homes, our abundance of food and comfort, all the things we have that most of the world does not. Our Thanksgiving Day feasts have thus become a subtle symbol of the fact that for vast numbers of us all of life has become a feast and that life itself is as lavish as the table we gather about on Thanksgiving Day.

If these were the basic reasons for giving thanks, then the only truly thankful people would be those who have it made. The unspoken assumption seems to be that the tougher life gets, the less thankful we can be. At its core, however, Thanksgiving should not be a celebration of abundance, but an expression of a hope and faith that sustains us even when outward circumstances are bad. In other words, Thanksgiving is not primarily about how much we have, but is about a way of looking at life even when we don't have much, or when our hearts are heavy and life is looking hard or hopeless.

What is it that enables me -- or you -- to be thankful rather than bitter even when life goes awry? What is it that enables us to be hopeful rather than despairing when things are not as we wish them to be? The ability to give thanks boils down to a matter of faith and hope -- a way of looking at life that moves beyond the outward circumstances which assail us all. In Tennyson's words, *"Well roars the storm to those that hear a deeper voice across the storm."* That's the only adequate way to explain what went on in Plymouth, Massachusetts, on the occasion of that first Thanksgiving feast. Those hardy souls had heard a deeper voice across the storm, and that made all the difference.

Year after year, our Presidents make Thanksgiving Proclamations. I want to share with you a somewhat different proclamation, this one by a friend and colleague, Arnold Kenseth. It goes like this:

> *Among Christians the one reason for thanksgiving is God himself. It cannot be otherwise, if we in any way understand our human situation: what frail and foolish, though often beloved, creatures we are; how we muddle after happiness; how we waste our substance in following shadows; how in the midst of plenty we are spiritually poor; how on the good green earth of God's providing we go about as joyless and hollow men. True, within the church we can 'count our blessings,' and 'go over the river and through the woods' with the sentimentalists; and we can nod our heads respectfully at the Pilgrims...sharing wild turkey with the Indians, and enjoy Kodachrome slides of red barns, silos, stacked corn, and pumpkins against the purple hills. Yet our thanksgiving can arise out of an assurance deeper than our human certainty, out of a blessing more eternal than the feast by which we celebrate, out of a power more majestic than New England Indian summer: namely, that it is God who gives us this land, it is God who provides us this feast, and it is God who saves us from ourselves for himself. Thanks be to God!*

Now *that's* a Thanksgiving Proclamation I can go along with.

* * *

GRACE NOTES

If the only prayer you say in your whole life is 'thank you,' that would suffice.
                                                    Meister Eckhart

When I was growing up, our family had a meal-time ritual. We would join hands around the table and sing a song of praise or thanksgiving. That we sang the same songs over and over did not seem to bother any of us very much. As I view this custom now, the point was not so much *what* we sang as *that* we sang. Each sung grace was an acknowledgement of the Source of life. Each was what Sam Keen has called a *"kneading of the vision of the sacred into the dough of everyday life."*

Later, when our own children were growing up, we continued the ritual, often using a simple spoken grace: "Thank you God, for food and family and friends." Eventually this prayer became rote and boring and we stopped doing it. Our children have long since grown up and left home, and with occasional exceptions my wife and I do not regularly observe this time-honored ritual of saying grace.

We are not sure that giving up the ritual was a good idea. In *Hymns to an Unknown God*, Sam Keen jolts me into re-thinking the question of saying grace. *"Our first priority for developing a spiritual practice,"* he writes, *"is the cultivation of a sense of gratitude and thanksgiving."* It doesn't matter whether we sing a song, speak a prayer, or simply observe a few moments of silent gratitude. Whatever way we choose, there is great value in the simple act of stopping to acknowledge the fact of our dependence on God and on the host of others who make our life possible. As Keen puts it, *"...an inspirited life is framed by gestures that interrupt the flow of profane time and punctuate our days with brief vistas of a transcendent reality."* Therefore, writes Keen,

Make a ritual of pausing frequently to appreciate and be thankful. Bless the food that nourishes you. Bless whoever loves you in any way. Bless the gifts and talents that call you to create. Bless the colors, one by one....Bless old friends. Bless little children and ancient parents. Bless the fit of man and woman, and tongue and groove, and all the unguents of pleasure....Bless sleeping and waking. Notice that the more you become a connoisseur of gratitude, the less you are the victim of resentment, depression, and despair. Gratitude will act as an elixir that will gradually dissolve the hard shell of your ego...and transform you into a generous being.

Now *that's* what I call a grace note!

*   *   *

REMEMBERING HOW TO LIVE

One day just before Christmas, three things happened to me. First, as I approached the local post office, I saw a man screech into a parking space, leap out of his car and race across the street into the post office as fast as his short, fat legs could carry him. Out again he came, dashing back to his car. Then, to my astonishment, another car pulled up and the same thing happened again.

Neither of these two hustling men was what anyone would consider a quintessential athlete. Each looked like a prime candidate for pulled muscles or heart attacks. Each was well on his way to a Type-A Christmas, giving a whole new meaning to the phrase, "dashing through the snow." There was a hint of desperation about them. If they had ever learned how to live this season serenely, deeply or quietly, they appeared to have forgotten it.

Second, a friend reminded me of a quote by Henry David Thoreau: *"Only that day dawns to which we are awake."* That struck me as a timely word about how to approach Christmas. If I were to catch the true spirit of Christmas, I would have to wake up, open my eyes and in Thoreau's words, *"live in each season as it passes; breathe the air, drink the drink, taste the fruit...."*

Third, I received a Christmas letter from a friend who wrote, *"I would like to learn, or remember, how to live."* And I thought to myself, "Exactly!" *That's* what Christmas is all about -- learning, or remembering, how to live.

I'm sure some other things also happened that day, but these are the three I remember.

*   *   *

III. WALKING THROUGH THE VALLEY OF THE SHADOW

*"Down the Valley of the Shadow
Ride, boldly ride...."*
Edgar Allan Poe

*"Even though I walk through the valley of
the shadow of death, I fear no evil, for
thou art with me; thy rod and thy staff,
they comfort me."*
Psalm 23:4

WALKING IN THE VALLEY

Introducing Part III

Down the corridor of Children's Hospital in Boston, a man and a teen-age boy are approaching. The boy does not look well. Suddenly the boy stops, leans his head against the wall. His face contorts. Slowly, angrily, he beats his fists against the wall. The man stands quietly beside him, not interrupting. Recovering his composure, the boy again stands erect, tears on his cheeks. The man enfolds him in his arms. The boy, oblivious to the glances of passersby, allows himself to be embraced for a long moment. The boy and the man look hard into each other's eyes, then together turn and walk out of the hospital.

I was that man. The boy was my son. Even now, twenty years after his death, memories like this come from time to time and bring tears to my eyes.

Like countless others -- perhaps like you -- I have walked in the valley of the shadow. The darkest of those shadows was the death of our son, Mark, who, after twenty years, finally succumbed to the cystic fibrosis with which he had been born. There have been other shadows as well. At the age of twenty months, our first daughter was discovered to have a massive, malignant tumor. My wife, Bobbie, has had breast cancer and a mastectomy. Three years ago our second daughter gave birth to her first child, Noah, who, brain-injured during birth, is seriously compromised with cerebral palsy. Because the past is never behind me and is always under my feet, these experiences color everything I write.

In the reflections that follow, I will not dwell much on death and dying. However, I am convinced that to live fully we must be aware that all of us walk in the shadow. I refer not only to what the Psalmist calls "the shadow of death," but also to the shadows caused by any kind of pain, suffering, loss, disappointment or grief. We cannot avoid the shadows, but we can learn to live with them and discover the light. If there were no light, there would be no shadows. That's what these next few reflections are about.

* * *

BY SWEETNESS WE SURVIVE

Outside the picture window beside our dining table we hang a feeder for hummingbirds. With breathtaking speed they dart in to drink. Then in the blink of an eye they are gone. Even when deeply engaged in conversation, guests at our table invariably interrupt one another to say, "Oh, look! A hummingbird!" as if they have never seen one before. I know of no other bird that depends so exclusively on sweetness for survival.

On the day I am writing these words, life is not feeling particularly sweet. However, it is in the very midst of some of the least sweet times that I have experienced what Isaiah calls *"the treasures of darkness."* I do not mean to imply that the darkness itself is sweet. What I find, however, is that dark times often reveal what is most important in my life. At the very moment life is *least* sweet, I become most aware of what is *most* sweet. A friend dying of cancer, for example, told me of his newly-found appreciation for the beauty in the flowers by his bedside. He felt as if he was truly seeing flowers for the first time in his life, and his eyes were filled with wonder. This was a treasure that came out of darkness, a sweetness that came in the midst of a bitter turn in his life.

My wife and I lived for twenty years with the knowledge our son would die at a young age. Words cannot describe the darkness that came with that awareness. On the other hand, because of that knowledge, each birthday was infinitely more precious, each vacation infinitely more appreciated, each moment of health an almost tangible joy. We were experiencing "the treasures of darkness." We were surviving by a sweetness that was made known to us by the threat of loss.

Almost all the pains, sorrows and disappointments of my life have been shot through with sweetnesses. Sometimes I see the sweetness best only in retrospect, but it is always there -- no question about that. To *know* it is there and to taste it is to survive. If we are alert, we can recognize that the treasures are there all the time -- but we have to pay attention to them. Often it is our darkest experiences that make this possible.

* * *

64

'NO HIDIN' PLACE DOWN HERE'

I retired -- more or less -- at the age of sixty-two. I have a friend who took the leap at sixty-one. He tells me that one of the main reasons he took his early retirement early was to regain control of his life. That was also part of *my* hope. However, within months of my friend's retirement, his grandson, like mine, was brain-injured at birth, and the nightmare for his family began -- a major loss of control. Then his elderly in-laws went into sharp decline, and he and his wife were caught up in frequent medical crises requiring hours of phone calls, emergency rooms, hospitalizations, and hands-on care -- another major loss of control.

The same has been true for my wife and me. Within three months of our attempt to get back control by retiring, both my wife's parents became seriously ill. There were hospitals, nursing homes, wrenching decisions. and finally their deaths within three weeks of each other. Then came the closing of houses, distributions and disposals of belongings accumulated over ninety years. Soon after that, we were caught up in two serious crises in our church, both of which involved us day and night over a period of years. Then came the birth of our grandson, Noah, and his cerebral palsy.

Those of us who look forward to getting our lives under control in retirement -- or at any other time -- need to reflect on the reality that there is no such thing as getting life under control. Life doesn't work that way.

I remember a song we used to sing around campfires. It must have begun as a spiritual. It has often come to mind in recent weeks.

> *There's no hidin' place down here,*
> *There's no hidin' place down here.*
> *I went to the Lord to hide my face,*
> *And the Lord cried out, NO HIDIN' PLACE.*
> *There's no hidin' place down here.*

To expect to control life is to live with an illusion. As Bill Coffin once put it, you can't be *disillusioned* if you don't have illusions in the first place. In spite of this, I discover that I *still* long for more control over my life. However, because I am convinced dark times will come to us, often just when we want them least, I need to live with them by learning to flower where God plants me. I can let go of unrealistic expectations, seek to enjoy to the full those blessed moments when unexpected and unwanted interruptions cease, and then respond to the interruptions as graciously as I can.

Truly, there *is 'no hidin' place down here.'*

* * *

BAD THINGS AND GOOD PEOPLE

If God is God, He is not good.
If God is good, He is not God.
Archibald MacLeish
J.B.

A few days after word had spread among our friends that our new grandson had suffered serious brain injury during his birth, a friend stopped by to express her sympathy. I was working in our yard when she arrived. Without preliminary pleasantries, she came directly to the point. Lovingly, she took my face in both her hands and with deep feeling said, "*Why* does God make bad things happen to good people?" Somewhat more abruptly than either she or I expected, I responded, "You are making two questionable assumptions -- one is that I am 'good,' the other is that God was responsible for what happened."

I apologized for being so abrupt. Her sympathy meant a great deal to me, but her assumptions had hit a raw nerve. The question she asked was not new to me. As a pastor, I have heard it countless times. Why *does* God make bad things happen to good people? Why does God *allow* bad things? For that matter, why does God make *good* things happen to *bad* people? Theologians call it 'the problem of evil.' If there is a good, loving, all-powerful God, why does He/She cause, or allow, evil?

One common explanation is that if we, like God, could see the larger picture, we would understand that what appears to be evil at the moment is really not evil at all. God's will, this explanation says, is far beyond our understanding and the faithful believer will therefore simply accept whatever comes in trust that in the long run it will all turn out to be for good. In other words, Father/Mother knows best.

Another explanation is that evil is God's way of punishing us for our sins. Somewhere, somehow, we have fallen short, and God is calling us to account and, ultimately, to repent.

Though these two explanations have given sustenance

and hope to countless people over the ages, from my point of view, both fall tragically short. Let me explain.

I have spent countless hours in all kinds of hospitals. The most painful of those hours have been on children's wards. For hours on end I have been surrounded by the gut-wrenching coughs and failing bodies of children and young adults with cystic fibrosis -- one of whom was my son. I have also been exposed to dozens of little cancer victims, many of them bald, scrawny, in pain, stuck full of needles. tubes and drugs. To believe that all this is 'the will of God,' that God's infinite wisdom and love have decreed that these children must suffer these illnesses for some greater good, or to believe that these illnesses are punishments to them -- or to their parents -- for sins named or unnamed, is beyond credulity. To be told that, for whatever reasons, God 'made' these illnesses happen to these particular youngsters is, to me, totally unacceptable. I look at all these children and ask, '*This* is the will of God?' What kind of God would this be?

These questions, of course, go well beyond hospital wards for little children. They apply to all the holocausts of history; they apply to mass murders, and to innocent victims all over the world who happen to be in the wrong places at the wrong times; they apply to all human injustices. If God is in control, why does God cause or allow them to happen?

So I come to another conclusion altogether, one which many will no doubt consider misguided or even heretical. What if God is *not* in control? What if God is *not* responsible for everything that happens? Some people are horrified at the thought. They say to me, "Then God wouldn't be God," as though God and control are one and the same thing. Suppose that instead of defining God in terms of Power and Control, we define God as the New Testament does -- God is Love. Love, too, is powerful, of course, Love may even be the greatest force in the world, but it does not *control*.

For example, on the human level I might love my neighbor or my child with all my heart, soul, mind, and strength, but all the loving in the world will not prevent my child or my neighbor from suffering pain, cystic fibrosis, cancer, brain damage or death. Love is powerful, but it does not control.

The fact that my love does not prevent bad things from happening does not cause me to question the reality or the power of love. By the same token, if God is Love, we should not expect God to control everything and prevent bad things from happening. Love neither causes nor allows bad things to happen to good people. What Love does do is to strengthen, support, nurture, and sometimes to heal in the midst of all the 'evil' things that can happen to us as the result of human carelessness, selfishness, greed, genetic defects, or the laws of nature. Love operating in those arenas may do wonderful, even miraculous, things and bring unexpected good out of evil situations, but it does not control.

I have been asked whether my son's cystic fibrosis and my daughter's cancer made me angry at God. I answer, 'No, I am not angry at God for the simple reason that I have never for one moment believed that God had anything to do with making those bad things happen." Instead, in all these experiences God has been the source of whatever strength I found in the midst of it. Anger, yes. Anger at God, no. At least that is how it has been for me.

I do not claim to have the last word on the 'problem of evil.' For me, however, I begin by letting go of the notion of an all-powerful, totally-in-control God who either makes -- or allows -- bad things to happen to good people. My God does not *make* evil things happen. I reject that kind of God. Instead, I place my trust in an all-loving, all-present, all-knowing God who promises to be with me in the midst of whatever evil comes my way. That is a God I can worship and seek to love with all my heart, soul, mind and strength.

* * *

ON FEELING DEPRESSED

We were vacationing in a cabin on Lake Pemaquid near Muscongus Bay on the coast of Maine. The sun warmed me as I relaxed on the porch in my favorite green metal chair -- the one with a bit of bounce in it. A zesty novel in my lap, an osprey circling overhead with its sharp, brittle cry, the sound of wavelets lapping the shore -- what more could I ask?   On the beach below, my nine-year-old grandson and his best friend were playing happily, their voices clear and full of summer exuberance. My wife was also on the beach reading and keeping an eye on the boys. Two cabins away, directly in my line of sight, my daughter, Ann, and her husband, Dan, were quietly going about their morning chores, sweeping out their cabin, hanging out wet suits and damp towels, preparing for the day. Even though I was keenly aware of all of these good things happening around me, at some deep level I was untouched by them. Things that would normally have filled me with warmth were not getting through. Inside I felt helplessly bleak, flat, dead. Nothing excited me. I felt no exuberance, not even for things that have almost never failed to stir me. Even though my mind told me this deadness would not last, at that moment it felt terminal.

Depression, I thought to myself, is like death. There was no way to convince myself the feelings could ever change. All I had to go on was the memory of past experiences of recovery, but even the memory felt like an illusion. That is what is so insidious about depression. It has the power to neutralize and paralyze hope.

The only thing that seemed to cut through the bleakness was my wife's love, and even that worked only fleetingly. Perhaps God could help, I thought, so I prayed about my depression, but without much sense of satisfaction. I reminded myself that faith, hope, and love abide, but the greatest of these is Love. However, I knew, even as those words came to me, that if I were in a worse depression, -- what is termed a clinical depression -- it was unlikely that even faith, hope and love would be able to break through. In that event, all that would be left would be some of the medical drugs which are blessedly available today for those who find themselves beyond the reach of faith, hope, or love.

The next morning, I went out from the camp with my son-in-law for coffee and a sticky bun in a nearby town. In my depressive mood, the thought of this outing did not excite me, but opportunities to spend time with Dan are all too rare and having previously agreed on this little expedition, I didn't want to back out on it. So we went. The conversation was good. Being with Dan was pleasant and healing. By the time we returned to camp, my mood was lighter.

Later in the day, a long walk with my daughter along Muscongus Bay on a beauty-filled Audubon trail refreshed my spirit some more. By evening, life was beginning to feel better. Love, it seemed, had broken through. My prayers, earlier so unsatisfying, no doubt had helped as well.

By the time I woke the following day, the gloom had lifted. My senses were reawakened. I felt alive. A book of poetry excited and energized me. For example, there was a poem by Antonio Machado, which contained these words:

Oh turn and be born again, and walk the road,
and find once more the lost path.

I said to myself a heartfelt, "Yes!" Then came a poem by Rolf Jacobsen:

Let the young rain of tears come.
Let the calm hands of grief come.
It's not all as evil as you think.

Again, I said from my heart, "Yes!" Then these words by Juan Ramon Jimenez:

I have a feeling that my boat
has struck, down there in the depths,
against a great thing.
And nothing
happens! Nothing...Silence...Waves...
Nothing happens? Or has everything happened,
and we are standing now, quietly, in the new life.

It was as if everything I read that morning had been written just for me, and my ears were open to hearing them in a new way.

Returning home a few days later, I felt as though I had found a new quietness in my depths, a new life, a new beginning. Ideas were bursting in me. I got up twice in the night to write down thoughts I did not want to lose. Creative juices were flowing again. I was awake. I was alive.

How did this happen? I do not know. But it did happen. And the next time life feels empty and hopeless, as it no doubt will, this will be one of the memories that will help me keep hoping even when dark feelings are upon me.

* * *

GOD'S LIGHT WORKS WELL WITH SHADOWS

One Thursday in Holy Week we were visiting friends in Pennsylvania. That evening we went with them to a Maundy Thursday service at a church in Valley Forge. There, in that somber, shadowed service, I heard some words that have stayed with me ever since: *"Shadows,"* the minister said, *"are mystery's midwives."*

Midwives, of course, are those who assist at a birth. They themselves are not going through labor to deliver a new life. They are simply assisting. That evening in Valley Forge, the minister seemed to me to be saying that like midwives the shadows in our lives assist us in giving birth to something new. "God's light," he said, "works very well with shadows."

I think of dark, shadowed cathedrals I have visited, and I see in their dim interiors a startling contrast to the plain-glassed, bright, open feeling of the New England meeting-houses in which I have spent so much of my life. The darkened, shadowed church is a beautiful symbol. The shadows whisper of Mystery and Awe, while the bright New England meetinghouses which I love so much seem to reflect that which is clear and understandable.   On Maundy Thursday, however, as on Christmas Eve, even New England meetinghouses are dimly lit. On these occasions, awe and mystery are in the air.

Frederick Buechner speaks of what he calls the *"muffled presence of the holy,"* of images of Christ that are broken, partial and ambiguous. Shadows remind me that it is always thus, simply because I am human and my mental atmosphere is always polluted. Seldom, if ever, do I see with the total clarity I might prefer. Always and inevitably, I see through a glass darkly, ambiguously.

Of course, there are also moments of clarity, occasional glimmerings of truth and grace. Nonetheless, shadows are the way life is much of the time, and for me, at least, grace is often given birth in the shadowed times.. With that moment of grace comes the discovery that, yea, though I walk through the valley of the shadow of death -- or the shadow of anything else that feels dark and threatening -- I need fear no evil, for God is with me.

That is what I mean by the treasures of darkness. A light does shine, even in the dark, and that light is most visible and shines brightest in the dark. At least this has been so for me. The truth is, God's light works very well with shadows.

*   *   *

FACING WHATEVER COMES

A preacher friend of mine once began a sermon with these words: *"The experiences of life are never correctly read or fully known until God gets done with them. We do not always know when a particular condition is happy and favorable or when another is wretched and unfortunate."* To buttress his point, he told an ancient Chinese story:

An old man was living with his son at an abandoned fort on top of a hill. One day he lost his horse, and the neighbors came to express their sympathy. "How do you know this is bad luck?" the old man asked. A few days later, his horse returned with a number of wild horses. So his neighbors came again, this time to congratulate him. The old man again replied, "How do you know this is good luck?" With so many horses around, his son took to riding, and before long he fell and broke his leg. Once more the neighbors came to express sympathy. The old man was not to be moved. "How do you know this is bad luck?" he said. The next year there was a war, and because the old man's son was crippled, he did not have to go to the front.

Another friend began his sermon with a different question: "Why me?" Then he claimed this is a question everyone asks. Many people do -- but not everyone. I, for one, almost never ask it. Given the barrage of tragedies stalking all humankind, I am far more inclined to ask, "Why *not* me?" Why should I not be vulnerable to all the same sufferings that afflict others?

I see myself as somewhat like a boxer. A boxer in the ring knows he will get hit. It's part of the game. He does not consider that getting hit or hurt constitutes a betrayal by the universe, an aberration in the way things ought to be. He doesn't complain that being hit isn't fair. In fact, he would be more surprised if he *didn't* get hit. He never asks, "Why me?"

In a similar way, I have come to expect that blows will come. When they do, I am not surprised, nor do I feel betrayed by God. I have found that the hard times in life are easier dealt with if I can remember these two things: first, that the experiences of life are never correctly read or fully known until God -- and I -- get done with them; and second, that "Why me?" is a useless and irrelevant question. Having taken those two thoughts to heart, then one tries to accept whatever comes and meet it with courage and the best one has to give.

*   *   *

A LETTER TO JANE

Our grandson, Noah, came into this world in the most traumatic way possible. During his birth, he was seriously ogygen-deprived and suffered injury to his brain. The diagnosis is cerebral palsy. The trauma does not go away.

If there are blessings in such an event -- and there are -- many of them come from the love and shared wisdom of friends. I want to share one of those blessings with you. It came in the form of a letter to Noah's mother -- my daughter, Jane -- from her friend, David Comstock, who also had a son with what seemed at the time to present severe challenges. With their permissions, here are some excerpts:

From all that you have written -- about Noah's birth and about his first year -- it's obvious that your son is a person of grit and determination. If he does indeed have CP, he will have to work all his life to interpret and reveal himself to other people. It's good that he has you for a mom....

As I think about our experience...there was a definite two-step process that we went through. Both steps are essential and one without the other is incomplete. The first was realizing and coming to terms with the fact that our son wasn't 'perfect.' The second was discovering that he was. I don't know how to explain it much better than that. A person looks forward to the birth of a child and fantasizes about what he or she will be like and all the things that s/he will accomplish and how proud you will be. Then something happens like Noah's trauma...and you feel (I felt) angry, cheated, and, yes, ashamed (like what the hell's the matter with you that you couldn't produce a perfect baby?) You spend a lot of time wishing things were other than they are. Then you set about all the tasks that go with whatever the 'thing' is. Learning about it -- Reimagining and Refantasizing your life/future. Priming yourself to be your kid's advocate (Hurt him and you die!)

Somewhere in that process you get to know your child. He is NOT the person you imagined before he was born and he is NOT the Condition that he has. He is this totally different person who is being shaped by -- among other things -- the condition that he has. And guess what? He's perfect. And he's so strong and funny and compassionate and passionate.... And the supreme irony is that his strength and humor and compassion and passion are to some important degree the product of the 'thing,' the 'challenge' -- whatever you want to call it.

My experience is this -- if you can live through that experience and see what's happening and believe it -- that imperfection gives birth to perfection and that weakness gives rise to strength -- then believing in the resurrection is small potatoes by comparison....

"Stay well and love that perfect boy passionately....

We sometimes wonder whether the words we have to say to each other in hard times can help very much. We don't need to be as eloquent and articulate as Jane's friend, but never underestimate the power of love to speak through our inadequate words. Never hold back because 'I don't know what to say.' Most of the time we *don't* know what to say -- so say what you can. Love will take it from there.

* * *

ON SAYING YES TO LIFE

When our son died, we found in his wallet a piece of paper on which were printed these words:

Easter is an affirmation of our deepest intuitions, our simple, child-like Yes to life and our insistent No to death. Easter tells us we can trust our burning hearts. Listen to the fire in your heart. What does it say you are? Doesn't it say something like this: 'I am alive. I am a miracle of life itself. I am a miracle of God. Deeper than all my guilt and fear, I am able to give and receive love. I am valuable. I am part of creation. I am not meant for death while I live, or when I die. I am meant to live, to create, to grow, to expand, nurture, cherish life and not be afraid or indifferent, but passionate and compassionate.' Easter is an affirmation of that

74

Yes, that heart on fire in you. Trust it. Live it...nothing less.

Theodore Loder

Those words obviously meant something special to Mark. He never spoke of them to us, but he lived them to a remarkable degree. That little piece of paper became a gift to us and to the countless friends and acquaintances with whom we have shared it since. We find in these words a wonderful affirmation of our deepest intuitions, our Yes to life, and the invitation to trust it and live it --nothing less.

* * *

75

IV. GROWING OLDER

"It is no great thing to live long...
but it is a great thing to live well."
St. Augustine

"So we do not lose heart. Even though
our outward nature is wasting away, our
inner nature is being renewed
day by day."
II Corinthians 4:16

THE OTHER SIDE OF THE APPLE TREE

Introducing Part IV

Now I become myself.
It's taken time, many years and places....
May Sarton
Collected Poems, 1930-1993

No doctor has told me I am dying. I am not aware of any condition which qualifies as life-threatening -- none, that is, except my age.

I could just as well have written that previous sentence at the age of forty-five, or even twenty-five. If the experts are right -- and there is no reason to doubt them -- our bodies begin to decline in various ways when we are scarcely out of our teens. Life itself, it has been said, is a terminal illness. That fact takes on a whole new meaning as I reach my mid-seventies. Even in my early sixties I slowly became aware that in certain respects time was running out, that I was living in the afternoon of my life and it would not be long before it would be *late* afternoon.

For years, I talked about being in the second half of life. There came a time, however, when it felt more honest to call it the third-third of life. Then came the fourth-fourth and the fifth-fifth. The chances are excellent that I will be kicking around on this planet five years from now. Those chances diminish somewhat if I think in terms of ten years from now. For that matter, there is no guarantee I will be here tomorrow, let alone ten or fifteen years from now.

I see nothing morbid or depressing about any of this. I am not preoccupied with my mortality, though this awareness is part of the undercurrent of my days. My son died at twenty; my brother died at sixty; my mother died at sixty-nine; my father died at eighty. As a pastor, I officiated at the funerals of nearly six hundred people, many of them younger than I am now. So, as I grow older, death is part of my consciousness. Rather than feeling depressed by this, my awareness helps me treasure each day more. Though my body is declining, my spirit is not, nor my joy in even the littlest of things. All this becomes one more component in the over-all context of these reflections I am writing.

There is an additional component in my understanding of what it means to grow old. I can describe it best by telling of a dream I had in my late forties. This is the dream:

I am planting five apple trees on a hillside. I leave them there to grow. Many years later, I come back to see how they are doing. As I approach the hillside, there they are, side by side, in full bloom, marvelously rounded, a beautiful sight to behold. With great excitement, I run up the hill to view them more closely. I am shocked to discover that the back side of each tree, the hidden side, is bare and flat. On this hidden side there are no blossoms, no buds, few branches. The hidden side is completely undeveloped. Clearly I need to find some way of rounding out that undeveloped side, and I set to work to do that.

This dream became for me the symbol of the meaning of the second half of life. Like most of my contemporaries, I had worked hard and blossomed well. From all appearances, I had been 'successful' in almost every part of my life. Nonetheless, I was haunted by the feeling that something was missing. I didn't know what it was. I was restless, dissatisfied. Maybe, I thought, I could find something more fulfilling if I left the ministry. Perhaps life would be better if I moved to a new location. My preaching, my marriage, life itself felt flat. As Tolstoy once put it, life was going "meaninglessly well." Something had to change.

I knew a fellow-pastor who seemed unusually perceptive and sensitive to what was going on below the surface of people. I went to him with my concern. One thing led to another, and I soon found myself in counseling with a therapist who knew a great deal about the second half of life. To make a long story short, I discovered that rounding out the undeveloped side of the apple tree is what the second half of life is all about. Over the next few years, life took on a meaning I had never known before. I felt literally reborn.

The apple tree dream is the key. Not only the second half of life, but the fifth-fifth as well, is for developing those parts of myself that have not been allowed or encouraged to grow in the first half. For me, this is an overarching awareness of my days. I believe this is what God intends for us as we grow older. Martin Buber once said, ***"...to be old is a glorious thing when one has not unlearned what it means to 'begin.'"*** Now is a time to begin. This is a time to open my window and let more of life in. One need not wait so long as I did to let that happen. If you are over the age of forty and under the age of one hundred, now may be the time for you!

* * *

ON BEING EASIER TO CATCH

...age is opportunity no less
Than youth itself.

Henry Wadsworth Longfellow

An old dog was chasing an old cat. They were both walking! I don't like to admit this, not even to myself, but, like the dog and the cat, as I get older I get slower. I see numerous evidences of slippage. Walking up a hill causes me to breathe harder than in the past. There are unfamiliar aches and pains. I feel more vulnerable when walking on icy sidewalks. When I attempted to pass the eye test for my driver's license without wearing my glasses, I almost failed. I am not hearing quite so well as I used to. My mind often goes blank when trying to remember a name.

For the most part, I accept all these slippages as natural and inevitable, but part of me, at least, is at war with my aging. When I go to the local Wellness Center with its battery of treadmills, stationary bicycles, rowing machines, chest presses, and strengthening machines of all varieties, I watch young men and women, lithe and muscular, running gracefully and effortlessly on the treadmills and am assailed by pangs of envy.

In the midst of all this, I am encouraged by a minister named Ted Loder, who has given me a new slant on some of the realities of aging. He writes about the wear and tear of time on his body and how he is trying, reluctantly, to accept the fact that he is growing slower on the inclines. Then, instead of bemoaning this universal experience of physical slow-down, he offers a fresh perspective He writes,

So take me, God,
I'm slower now,
easier to catch,
and needy.

He then reflects on the possibilities of maintaining a youthful spirit in spite of his aging body, asking God to help him be

...aware of what young truly is:
eager, curious, dauntless,
willing to explore, to struggle,
to be foolish as the world goes,
foolish, caring, trusting, open,

and brave....
Wrestling the Light

So, I am getting older. I know the years ahead of me are far fewer than the ones behind me. Partly because I know that my years are limited, I find them increasingly precious and want to find ways to live them with all the joy and hope that is available to me. As Doris Grumbach once put it, **"*I am not happier with what I have...but I am more grateful for what I have left.*"** One of the ways I can achieve this is to focus on what I *can* do rather than on what I *cannot* do and to look for those things this phase of life offers me that earlier stages did not -- including the fact that in my relationship with God, I may now be easier to catch.

* * *

SENIOR MOMENTS

We've still got all our marbles. We just can't remember where they are.
> Source unknown

We 'seniors' like to joke about what are affectionately called senior moments -- those embarrassing lapses of memory when we cannot recall a familiar name or find the right word. Frustrating as those moments are, clearly one of the best ways to deal with them is laughter.

Recently, my wife and I took a trip to New Mexico to visit the Carlsbad Caverns and other sights along the way. My sister, who was traveling with us, brought a tape recording of a speech by Ram Das about the process of growing older. So as we drove those long Southwestern miles, we listened to his wisdom and the frequent laughter of his audience. Because I find it helpful to laugh at some of the common results of aging, I want to share two humorous verses he quoted. I think you will enjoy them most if you read them aloud, even if no one else is present to hear them.

> *It's not the crow's feet under your eyes*
> *That make you old,*
> *Or the gray in your hair, I'm told.*
> *But when your mind makes a contract your body*

can't fill,
You're over the hill, buddy, you're over the hill.

Just a line to say I'm living
That I'm not among the dead,
Though I'm getting more forgetful
And mixed up in the head.
I can't remember, when I stand at the foot of the
    stairs,
If I must go up for something
Or if I've just come down from there.
And before the fridge, so often, my poor mind is
    full of doubt,
Have I just put food away, or have I come to take
    some out?
And there are times when it is dark out, and with
    my nightcap on my head
I don't know if I'm retiring, or just getting out of
    bed.
So if it's my turn to write you
There's no need in getting sore.
I may think that I have written,
And don't want to be a bore.
Remember I do love you,
And I wish that you were here.
And now it's nearly mail time,
So I'll say goodbye, my dear.
There I stood before the mailbox
With my face so very red,
Instead of mailing you my letter,
I opened it instead.
I love my new bifocals,
My dentures fit me fine.
My hearing aid is perfect,
But Lord, I miss my mind!

The audience exploded with laughter. But why? *This* is
funny? Alzheimer's is funny? Losing one's mind is funny?
The mere thought of it is devastating. So what's the laughter all
about? The best explanation is that this is combat humor. Some
of the best jokes and cartoons during World War II came out of
the nightmare of combat. Sometimes the only way to survive the
nightmare was to find humor in the midst of it. So, we elderly
laugh -- when we can -- at what we see happening to us and

those we love.   And we pray mightily that the day may never come when we have to say, "But Lord, I miss my mind." At the same time we pray for grace to be compassionate toward those whose minds have really let them down.   They can't help it. Poignant, sad, heart-rending? Yes. But never, never funny.

*   *   *

IN DEFENSE OF GEEZERDOM

Few people consider it a compliment to be called an "old geezer." Our grandson, David, recently reminded me of this.   His father had invited him on a trip to visit some elderly relatives in western Minnesota. He promised David that en route they would have opportunities to see large flocks of snow geese.   To David's disappointment, a large flock of elderly relatives turned out to be more in evidence than the snow geese. On their way back to Minneapolis, David complained to his father, "I thought you said we would see geese, not geezers!" Clearly, geezers did not rank highly on David's list.

Not long after that episode was reported to us, my wife and I had had an unusually full week and were looking for a bit of relaxation.   Perhaps a movie would do. We decided on *Waking Ned Devine.*   One of the most delightful characters in the film turned out to be an old man who, in the words of film critic, Roger Ebert, had arrived at *"...the ultimate reaches of geezerdom."* This old man, says Ebert, *" ...with his twinkling eyes and turkey neck, is engaging, conspiratorial, and delighted by all things not too wicked."*   He was all of that and more. Geezerdom was beginning to take on an aura of delight rather than boredom.

The next day, rummaging around in our family archives, I discovered an envelope containing a small stack of my mother's old letters. Folded into one of those letters was a small piece of cardboard about three by four inches in size.   There, in tiny, but legible handwriting, were two light-hearted poems about the upside of geezerdom. Here they are:

After Seventy

Pamper the body,
Prod the soul,
Accept limitations,

But play a role.
Withdraw from the front,
But stay in the fight.
Avoid isolation,
Keep in sight.
Beware of reminiscing
Except to a child.
To forgetting proper names
Be reconciled.
Beware of loquacity,
Be crisp and concise,
And regard self-pity
As a cardinal vice.
Oliver Higgins Prouty

I'm Old in Years

I'm old in years as the records go,
No use denying that is so.
But I've young ideas
And a gleam in my eye,
And I still want ice cream
On top of my pie.
Anonymous

So, let's hear it for all old geezers who are *"...engaging, conspiratorial, delighted by all things not too wicked,"* who stay in the fight with young ideas and a gleam in their eye, and still want ice cream on top of their pie. Perhaps I could even become one of them!

* * *

FALLEN MONUMENTS

Most of us hope that when we die we will leave something of ourselves behind by which, with a bit of luck, others will remember and honor us. For some that might be a book, for some a building with our name on it, for some a successful business. For others it might be children, or the passing on of a family name. Unfortunately, this dream does not always come true.

I do not recall ever having had a conscious ambition to leave monuments by which people would remember me. Now, in retirement years, however, I am startled to discover that in fact I *do* harbor some wish that the churches I served, for example, would so thrive, grow and prosper that folks might say to each other -- or I might even say to myself -- "That's the church Tuck Gilbert helped to build -- what a great job he did!"

However, such is not likely to be the case. For all I know, my first parish, which, like a first love, will always be special in my memory, may not even exist any more. It left the denomination which gave it birth and supported it generously through its infancy. If it still exists, there are few there, if any, who will remember me at all. Whatever it has become is vastly different, I am sure, from anything I ever envisioned for it. No monument there.

Another of my favorite churches has been through years of turmoil and change. It has moved in directions I could never have foreseen, bearing little resemblance now to my vision for it over thirty years ago. No monument there.

Within three years of my leaving, the church I served longest, loved best and consider my most fruitful effort, was devastated by a serious controversy. Though the congregation has healed well and under superb leadership has come back together, much of the groundwork that was laid during my years there has been re-plowed, re-furrowed and re-seeded -- as it ought to have been. There are very few outward signs remaining of what I thought of as my special contribution to it. I will always love that church and its people, and will forever treasure the years I was privileged to serve there. However, whatever hopes I may have held secretly-- even from myself -- it never was and never will be a monument.

So I am like the farmer who knows that no matter how well he plows, seeds and fertilizes, and no matter how much fruit his efforts bear, in autumn the fruits of his labor will all be cut to the ground. No matter how excellent and useful they may have been, they no longer stand. No monuments there. This is a lesson the vast majority of us will someday have to learn. My guess is that most of us will not learn this lesson until our retirement years, just when we need to know that our life-work mattered, that our efforts made a difference and that we are still worthy of respect.

So it can be a tough lesson -- *and* the beginning of wisdom! In the end, as Paul puts it in his first letter to the Corinthians, **"...faith, hope and love abide, these three; but the greatest of these is love."** *(I Corinthians 13:13)* Love does not fall nor fail. When all is said and done, if we are to be measured at all, it will be not by how well we built, not by how hard we worked or how much we achieved, but by how well we loved.

* * *

A LIGHT-HEARTED DEATH WISH

I once spent a summer as one of the chaplains in a nursing home. I naively made the assumption that being frail in body and sometimes in mind, many of these mostly elderly folks would be feeling fearful about dying. So, when it seemed appropriate, I would sometimes ask, "Are you afraid of dying?" More often than not the answer, though not necessarily in these exact words, was , "No, I'm afraid of *not* dying."

Some years later, I was privileged to know a woman many years my senior who put this fear into poetry. She had reached a point where, with body and eyes failing and the years accumulating far beyond the average, she wrote the following words:

A Light-hearted Death Wish

Old heart, dear friend, it is time to say,
(Though you still are ticking in the same old
* way,)*
That your work is done. Be still.

You've empowered my hands. They have made
* my bed,*
Written my letters and baked my bread.
They are crippled now. Be still.

The limbs and feet that have borne my weight
Resist my using them much of late.
Do you get my point? Be still.
Once crowded with sprightly thoughts, my
* mind*
May have them still but they're hard to find.
I miss them so! Be still.

Why in the world should you keep on ticking
When my vital parts have taken a licking.
I'm pleading now. Be still.

87

No need to answer. Just...be...still.

Lois Grant Palches

Her plea has been granted. Her heart is still. And I will never again make the false assumptions I brought to that nursing home years ago.

* * *

AN ANCIENT MAPLE TREE AND A QUESTION

On a hillside in Vermont there is an ancient maple tree at the edge of a pasture. Year after year, my sister visited that tree, leaned against it, touched and felt its majesty and strength. One year, to her distress, she found its center had begun to rot. Sensing the vulnerability and finiteness of that great tree, she asked a question: "What good is height if roots and center fail?"

Especially for children, height is a very basic issue. I have clear memories of a childhood birthday ritual. Each birthday my mother would back me up against the wall, place a ruler on my head and record my height with a pencil mark and a date. With great pride I would compare that mark with previous ones, delighted with my new height. When my wife and I became parents, we did the same with our children. We like to think that height is a mark of growth and maturation. But, as my sister asks, what good is height if roots and center fail?

We don't need a child, a ruler and a birthday for the asking of this question. Now, in the fourth-fourth of my life, the question seems even more relevant than it did when I was young. Now, more than ever, the measure of my growth is not based on anything outward. What counts are roots and center.

I am sure this is what Paul means when he writes, *"Even though our outer nature is wasting away, we are being inwardly renewed."* (*II Corinthians 4:16*) At seven or at seventy, that's what roots and center are all about.

* * *

88

WHAT LESSONS HAVE I LEARNED?

When the world was preparing for the turn of the century, I assigned myself five questions to reflect upon:
1. What will I want to leave behind as this century closes?
2. What will I wish to carry forward with me into the new century?
3. What lessons have I learned thus far?
4. What have been the most significant events of my life-time?
5. What memories or yearnings will there be in my heart when, on Christmas Eve, I sing, "The hopes and fears of all the years are met in thee tonight?"

This was not an easy assignment, but it was a good one. For me, the toughest question turned out to be the third -- what lessons have I learned thus far? However, this is an appropriate end-of-year question and would be equally so for a birthday or any other day in the year. Here are some of the lessons I wrote in my journal:

- There is more to everything than meets the eye.
- Honesty really is the best policy. But there are exceptions.
- In human relationships *trust* is everything. Breaking trust creates an almost insurmountable barrier.
- "Fair" is not a working principle in the universe. Don't expect it to be. Pain, suffering, grief, hurt and tragedy happen to everyone, and usually they aren't "fair."
- *All* humans have a 'dark' side. There is little of evil in this world that I am not capable of doing under the right -- or wrong-- circumstances.
- *All* humans have a 'light' side. There really *is* such a thing as 'higher angels' in everyone. Some call it the 'image of God,' or the 'spark of divinity.'
- The scientific world-view is seriously limited. There are realities it cannot deal with, and the full life requires us to deal with those other realities.
- Death is not the worst thing that can happen to me.
- To assume that apparently rational people will necessarily behave rationally is itself irrational.
- When smart people do stupid things, one can assume that powerful forces are unconsciously at work.

89

- There are very few absolutes. And whereas there *are* Absolutes, human beings cannot know the Absolute absolutely.
- There is always -- or almost always -- at least more than one side to a point of view and probably some truth in both.
- The moment I think I know the whole truth about anything, I should start to look for arguments on the other side.
- No religion has the whole truth. Most religions have some of the truth.
- Beware of extremists no matter whose side they are on.
- Some of the most Christ-like people in this world are not Christians.
- Some of the least Christ-like people in this world call themselves Christians.
- Gratitude is a major virtue. Generosity comes close behind.
- Guilt is not always a bad thing. It is the inevitable consequence of a sensitive conscience.
- The remedy for guilt is not to develop self-esteem, but to lay hold of the conviction of a Higher Power who forgives and accepts us as we are.
- Love is the operative principle in life. It supersedes all laws and rules of human behavior.
- Inclusive is almost always better than exclusive.
- What really matters is not what happens to me, but how I deal with what what happens to me.
- Bad things happen to 'good' people -- *and* to 'bad' people.
- Good things happen to 'bad' people -- *and* to 'good' people. Good things and bad things have little or nothing to do with reward and punishment.
- The best way to become aware of the lessons I have learned is to make a list!
- No list of lessons learned will ever completely describe what I have learned.

That was part of the list I wrote late in 1999. I do not expect you will agree with all the things I think I have learned. The question is, what lessons have *you* learned?

* * *

90

V. RELATIONSHIPS

*Love alone is capable of uniting living beings
in such a way as to complete and fulfill them,
for it alone takes them and joins them by what
is deepest in themselves.*
> **Pierre Teilhard de Chardin
> in *The Phenomenon of Man***

BEING MARRIED

Introducing Part V

In the next few pages you will find some reflections about marriage, parenting and other relationships. Perhaps the most important thing I can say about myself as context for these reflections is the fact that in August, 2003, Bobbie and I will have been married fifty years. We will continue that relationship 'till death us do part.'

For over twenty years, the two of us have led communication workshops and retreats for married couples. We often tell those couples that we have each been married at least six times. We have had one wedding, but several marriages. This is our way of reminding couples that over the years relationships change. Multiple shifts and transitions have to be lived through. When we move from one stage to another, we enter a relationship that is sometimes so different from the previous one that it is like a whole new marriage. Such changes often upset the delicate balances of a marriage. Finding new balances that work can take a great deal of time and intentional work. Couples have often told us that this simple concept is one of the things they remember and appreciate most about our workshops..

With all of its changes -- and partly *because* of those changes -- our marriage has provided many of our richest and most precious experiences in life. That is not to say it has always been easy. Survival has its roots in a love and loyalty that carry us through the best of times and the worst of times. That is what these next few reflections are about.

*   *   *

ONE CANDLE, TWO FLAMES

"Marriage is that relation between man and woman in which the independence is equal, the dependence mutual, and the obligation reciprocal."

Louis Kaufman Anspacher
in an Address, at Boston,
December 30,1934

A popular ritual at weddings is a symbolic act performed by the bride and the groom. Separately, each lights a taper from an altar candle. Together, they then light the single wick of a marriage candle, their two separate flames thus merging into one. What do they then do with their two separate flames? They blow them out!   Good Lord! They extinguish the symbol of their separateness!

Though I know this ritual has seemed very beautiful and moving to many, I have consistently discouraged its use. I ask couples to *think* -- to think what that symbolic gesture really says. I suggest to them that it seems to imply that marriage requires us to snuff out individuality, whereas marriage should *preserve* individuality rather than destroy it.

Most couples quickly grasp my point, and for them I propose a simple, but profound, shift in the imagery. Instead of lighting a single flame, I encourage them to create their own marriage candle -- a single candle with two wicks -- so that even as they unite, they retain their sense of separate identities symbolized by one candle with two flames.

The longer I am married -- nearly fifty years now -- the truer and more important that symbol seems to me.

* * *

"BLOW ON THE COALS OF MY HEART"

Curious about our workshops and retreats for married couples, people sometimes asked, "Are you marriage counselors?" "No, we're not marriage counselors." "Well, then, what *do* you do?" "We teach communication skills," or, "We teach conflict management," or, "We help couples learn intimacy," we would reply. None of these explanations felt quite right. Then, one day, we received a mimeographed letter from an Oberlin College student who was serving for a year in Indonesia. His letter gave us the words we were looking for to explain what we were doing with those couples' groups. Here, slightly adapted, is a portion of what he wrote after returning from a solo camping expedition to Mount Rinjani:

Two fatal flaws when building fires in perpetually wet environments: 1) underestimating the value of kindling, and 2) thinking that there is some point, some critical mass of heat and light after which the fire could not possibly go out. No such point exists -- even the largest bonfire can be snuffed due to inattention.

The small stuff is essential. After the first day I had built up a good supply of logs of forearm thickness, but every morning saw me out after twigs. A handful of good dry bark-stripped twigs is far more essential to the future of a fire than any number of big sticks you can drag to camp. The twigs I would bring into the tent with me. They are that important.

But keeping a fire lit at Rinjani is a bit like singing a call-response spiritual. There can be 80 verses, but you always come back to the same line, the same chorus: blow on the fire. Anything you do, at any time, the most immediate need is brought home to you: blow on the fire, keep it going. Find the flashlight and the noodle packs, blow on the fire. Spread the tarp, locate the cup, blow on the fire. Walk down to water side, clean the cup, walk on back, blow on the fire. Sit a minute, smile, look for constellations in the open sky, blow on the fire. Get out the knife, open the package, blow on the fire. Separate out the flavor packs, wipe your eyes, blow on the fire.

I have always had a difficult relationship with fire....At the same time, I've always had difficulty keeping friendships strong. Analogous problems, I now realize: underestimating the small stuff, and assuming that there's some point after which the blaze just burns on and on forever.

Peter Riggs

That's what we do, my wife and I said to each other. We teach couples to blow on the fire! The metaphor, of course, fits not only marriage, but friendship, parenting, any human relationships that matter. Always, always, there is the need to recognize the importance of 'the small stuff,' and to know that there is no point after which the blaze just burns on forever and ever without being fed and blown upon.

* * *

WHEN LOVE TAKES ALL YOU'VE GOT (PART I)

There is no more lovely, friendly, charming relationship, communion, or company than a good marriage.

Martin Luther

I often begin a wedding ceremony with these words: *"We come together to celebrate and to record in the minds and hearts of all present the joyous event of a love that has grown. We gather also to mark the reality that marriage is not easy and that along with the tenderness, hope, and joy a marriage must rise above and work through difficulties, misunderstandings, and barriers of many kinds."* Celebration, yes -- by all means -- but also the recognition, right from the start, that marriage is not easy, that love takes all we've got.

In spite of an abundance of the blessings and joys of love, the relationships of marriage and parenthood are fragile. The only ones who do not know this are the young, the naive and the inexperienced. The rest of us -- those who are separated or divorced, those who fear that they will eventually be divorced, those who hope they soon will be divorced and those who are married reasonably happily and expect to stay that way -- all know that even the most loving of human relationships are tender, fragile and easily damaged or broken.

That is why every wedding ceremony should acknowledge that the marriage relationship is not easy, that it takes all we've got, *and* that it promises more glimpses of heaven than any other relationship we are likely to know on earth.

* * *

96

WHEN LOVE TAKES ALL YOU'VE GOT (PART II)

I once knew a young couple who were quite awed by the fact that they were about to celebrate their 10th wedding anniversary. None of their friends, they said, had made their marriage last that long. That young couple, no longer young, are still together after nearly thirty years.

Not long ago I helped dear friends celebrate their fiftieth anniversary. We recently attended a relative's sixtieth. How *do* people make marriage last that long? Pure dumb luck? A rare and happy blend of compatible personalities? Hard work? Grace? Some combination of the above? Or, as some people believe, is a long-lasting marriage simply a mystery?

My wife and I would probably answer, "All of the above." For us, certainly, there has been some luck along with a happy blend of personalities. Even more important, we have both been flexible and willing to adjust to each other's needs, wishes and quirks. Hard work? Definitely. Hours of good, hard, honest, and sometimes painful talk with each other about needs and feelings as we attempt to respond in constructive ways to our differences -- in other words, the willingness and ability to talk, to listen, to be honest, to engage in give-and-take. Grace? Of course, grace being the undeserved and often unexpected gift of love, acceptance, support and forgiveness both from each other and from God. So, yes, all these are part of the explanation of how a marriage survives the test of time.

There are two more qualities which, though less tangible, undergird all the rest: one is love; the other loyalty. By love, I do not mean the *feeling* of 'being in love' -- though that certainly helps -- but rather the decision and commitment to treat each other in loving ways even when one's mood is not particularly loving. Some people might call this respect.

When I officiate at weddings, I usually include the following words: *"As you stand in the presence of God, remember that love and loyalty alone will avail as the foundation of a happy and enduring home."* Those words point, I believe, to the primary reason our marriage has survived the years. To over-simplify a bit, love makes for a *happy* home; loyalty makes for an *enduring* home -- loyalty being the down-deep commitment to hang in there together when the feelings of love waver, weaken or grow dull. Loyalty is the glue that helps us persevere in finding a way through times of dullness, friction, disappointment, and the sense of being stuck in 'Holy Deadlock.' Having made a basic commitment for the long haul, our own self-interest compels us to find a way to make the

97

marriage work -- to recover the life, the love, the vitality in our relationship. Loyalty prevents our giving up. Then love, given a fair chance, is provided the gift of time to recover, to return, to resurface, to be reborn.

I wouldn't bet a nickel on any marriage in which there is little or no commitment to love *and* to loyalty. After Grace and Mystery, they are the bottom line.

* * *

WHAT'S *NOT* WRONG?

One morning, in a particularly negative mood, I was brought up short by the words of Thich Nhat Hanh, a Vietnamese Buddhist monk. We so often ask, *"What's wrong?"* he said, when we *could* be asking *"What's not wrong?"* Even in my negative mood, I found I could easily name quite a list of things about myself, my wife, my life, the world that were *not* wrong. To my surprise, the question worked. I began to feel better.

A few mornings later, I came across Ralph Waldo Emerson's words: *"Every Man is entitled to be valued by his best moments."* (Emerson, unfortunately, was not aware of the virtue of inclusive language!) To my surprise that one worked also. I am conditioned, it seems, to focus on my worst moments -- or at least my less-than-best ones -- and to judge myself accordingly. I was feeling down on myself that particular morning, and that brief sentence of Emerson's jolted me out of my negativity. I am entitled to be valued by my best moments. What a relief! My wife is also entitled to be valued by her best moments. Another relief. My minister is entitled to be valued by his best moments. Another relief. My President is entitled to be valued by his best moments. Another relief.

There is a potentially transforming and life-giving gift in those two chance encounters with a Buddhist priest and a Concord philosopher -- "What's *not* wrong?" and "All are entitled to be valued by their best moments."

I find it helpful to remind myself of this gift each day.

* * *

"WHAT'S FORGIVENESS, MOMMY?"

One New Year's Eve, Grandma, Grandpa, their daughter, Ann, and her son, David, went to the early portions of a First Night celebration in Keene, New Hampshire. When it came time to go home, three-and-a-half-year-old David decided he was not ready to leave, but Grandma, Grandpa and Mommy were not dissuaded. Determined not to cooperate, David stiffened his little body to prevent these three equally determined adults from inserting him in his car seat. Tension began to build. After a rigorous struggle, he was finally strapped in safely, and we began the half-hour journey home. Frustrated and angry, David began to beat on his mother with his little fists. Refusing to put up with this, she grasped his wrists in one hand and held him off while I drove. In the back seat, the needle on the tensionometer was rapidly moving into the red danger zone.

A long, tense silence was finally broken by a question from David. "Mommy, what's forgiveness?" Taken off-guard by the question, his mother nevertheless gave him a brief, off-the-cuff, simple definition. I couldn't have done better if I'd had a week to think about an answer. Now another silence while he digested this information. Once again it was David who spoke first, this time with an announcement: "Mommy, I *don't* forgive you." Now that he knew what forgiveness was, it was perfectly clear to him -- he didn't forgive.

Unforgiven Mommy kept a firm grip on his little wrists. We were definitely in the red zone now. We pulled into the garage in silence. The moment the car stopped, Mommy was out of the car in a flash, into the house, and into her bedroom, closing the door behind her. Mommy had had it! This was definitely *not* a good way to spend New Year's Eve!

Grandma, a creative, non-anxious presence in a tense situation, lifted David out of his car seat and before he knew what was happening stripped him of his clothes, plunked him into a tub of nice warm water, and sat with him until his skin was pinked and pruned. Gradually he relaxed and began to talk. Soon he came to a conclusion: "I'll forgive *her* if she'll forgive *me*."

"Why don't you tell that to Mommy?" Grandma asked. David did. Mommy did. Then, quite happy, we all went to bed.

* * *

99

WHEN I FIND IT HARD TO FORGIVE

Forgiveness is not always easy for me. When the hurt is a minor one or is caused by someone not close to me, forgiving is relatively easy. However, when I have experienced a major hurt caused by someone to whom I feel close, someone I have trusted, then forgiveness is much more difficult.

I am thinking of a painful rift I experienced in a relationship that mattered to me. It happened like this: a close friend; a misunderstanding; angry and accusing words that cut to the quick; wounds too deep and painful to be lightly dismissed even if there were an apology, which there never was. Something had been broken.

Even though I am convinced that forgiveness is the only way to heal that kind of break, the willingness and ability to act on this conviction have often been difficult. In *The Return of the Prodigal Son,* Henri Nouwen confesses that for him *"Forgiveness from the heart is very, very difficult. It is next to impossible....I have often said, 'I forgive you,' but even as I said those words my heart remained angry or resentful...I still wanted to hear apologies...."* Though apologies can soften the pain, when a hurt has been profound and the break has been seriously damaging, an apology will not do the trick. Something more is required. That something is forgiveness, which I define as 'love acting to heal a break.'

Here are five things I have learned about those times when I find forgiveness difficult.

1. There has to be a deep desire to heal the wound or the break. The relationship has to be so important to me that the break *matters* greatly.

2. Forgiveness requires patience. If the relationship really matters and the hurt has been major, forgiveness probably will take time -- maybe months, or even years. The healing cannot be hurried or forced.

3. Healing begins with confession -- *my* confession, that is. I must look *inward* to *my* part in the break, however unwitting or unconscious it may have been. This, for me at least, has been head and shoulders above every other step in freeing me from whatever hurts and angers are blocking my openness to healing. Clinging to my anger is a mighty temptation. However, the longer I hang onto my anger, the more damage I do to myself. I have found that confession is the quickest and surest way to counteract this danger.

4. I need to let go of who's right and who's wrong. In that contest, there are no winners. Leave it alone. It leads nowhere.

5. Finally, I find I need to do a great deal of praying. I need to pray for the person who has hurt me. I need to pray for myself. I need to pray for the relationship. I need to do everything in my power to look at all this through God's eyes -- to see the situation as God does. Prayer is the most available way to do that.

There are no guarantees the broken relationship will ever be the same again. Nonetheless, in Henri Nouwen's words, *"Life is an adventure in forgiveness."* These five steps, I believe, are the surest ways to begin the adventure.

* * *

A MESSAGE ON A LICENSE PLATE

On a hot summer afternoon, coming off Memorial Drive in Cambridge, Massachusetts, I found myself stuck in traffic. With nothing else to do, my eyes finally settled on the license plate on the car ahead of me. I am an inveterate watcher of license plates. I have spotted HAVUD -- obviously a proud alumnus of a famous university. I have seen CONCUD, for nearly eighteen years my home town with a Boston accent. One summer in Maine I saw a Massachusetts car with BAHABA on its plate, a Bay Stater who liked to vacation in Bar Harbor, no doubt. But here, right before my eyes, was something more intriguing. URUIMI, was what I saw. I was momentarily baffled. Then it dawned on me. You Are You; I am I.

I took that wonderfully helpful message home with me that day, and at least for a short time, I was a better husband, a better father, and a better pastor. I became, at least for the moment, more respectful of the differences in our personalities, beliefs, perspectives, and values.

The key for me is the word, 'respectful.' The fact that we differ from one another is not a problem in and of itself. Trouble begins when we cease to *respect* the differences. One of the qualities I have come to admire most in couples is not compatibility, but respectfulness in the midst of incompatibilities.

In preceding reflections, I have praised the qualities of love, loyalty, and forgiveness as the conditions for happy and long-lasting relationships, not only between couples, but between friends, colleagues and fellow church members. I here add respect. That chance encounter with a lowly license plate on the streets of Cambridge has been a gift to me. I need that respectful reminder that you are you and I am I, and that is how it is meant to be.

* * *

YOU ARE A MARVEL

If only there were someone to lean over every crib and whisper into every new pair of ears, 'God is!'
Elizabeth O'Connor
in *Cry Pain, Cry Hope*

When we brought our first baby home from the hospital, her grandmother was there to greet us. We gently laid the baby in her crib, and the three of us -- father, mother, and grandmother -- stood quietly, gazing in wonder at this new little being. Then the grandmother said, "Don't you think we should say a prayer?" So we did. I probably would not have said that prayer -- at least not aloud -- if my mother-in-law had not suggested it, but I have always been glad she did.

Pablo Casals asks a question which, if you are not inclined to pray aloud, may be more your cup of tea:

When will we teach our children...who they are? We should say to them: Do you know who you are? You are a marvel. You are unique. In all the world there is no other child exactly like you. In the millions of years that have passed there has never been another child like you.   And look at your body -- what a wonder it is....

In *Joys and Sorrows*

In short, when a child is born, reverence and awe are the order of the day. Whether we respond with a spoken prayer or with Casals' questions, we are on the right track. However, when a child is born, most of us will find ourselves asking an additional question: "What will this child become?" Casals suggests we say to the child, *"You may become a Shakespeare, a Michelangelo, a Beethoven. You have the capacity for anything. Yes, you are a marvel. And when you grow up, can you then harm another who is, like you, a marvel?"*

We never know, of course, who or what a child may

102

become.   But I think we do the child no favor when we say, "You have the capacity for anything."   The truth is we cannot all be Shakespeares, Michelangelos or Beethovens. That is asking too much.   We cannot ask or expect our children to become *more* than they they have it in them to become.

When I was young, I sometimes felt that my parents expected me to be *more* than I was capable of being, that I was a disappointment to them when I fell short of their dreams and expectations for me.   But that is entirely different from saying, "Do you know who you are?   You are unique.   You are a marvel!" -- such a marvel, in fact, that we will lean over their cribs and whisper, 'God is!'

*   *   *

THERE MUST HAVE BEEN A STAR

Was there a star that night I was born?
Can you remember, Mother?
Once you told me
the pale naked fingers of grey morning
were just creeping across the wall
when you first heard me cry.
But what about that star, was there a star?
Faint, cold, and pale in lonely space,
Or red and burning across the wasteland of the
sky - or, perhaps no star at all?
No, no, there must have been a star....
                    Written by a 17-year-old girl, anonymous

Of course there was a star!   There was a star the night our first child was born, and the second, and the third. I didn't have to go out into the night to see for myself, but I know there *must* have been. For *every* parent, when a child is born, there is a star, a dream, a hope for that child.

Was there a star the night that I was born? If so, what did it stand for in the hearts of my mother and father? What was the hope, the dream that accompanied my birth?   For good or ill, these are powerful, poignant questions, shapers of a child's life.
What do *you* hope for the children of your seed, your womb, your heart? What is your hope for the children of your community, your friends, your world? Some people hope and pray their children will make it on the fast track, that they will be

103

successful, that they will go, let's say, to Harvard or Yale.

Because of the circumstances of my birth -- a British ship in war-torn Chinese waters, a British doctor, German, Czechoslovakian and Chinese nurses -- my parents dreamed that I would be an instrument of peace, an influence for internationalism and love in the world.

What is *your* hope? What does that star stand for? Does it stand for stardom or for servanthood? Does it stand for commitment to some great cause or for service to humanity? Does it stand, perhaps, for strength of faith, or moral courage, or personal integrity? Does it stand for unselfishness, thoughtfulness, honesty and sensitivity?

There is an even more important question: do we have any right at all to hold a dream for a child, even if it is for something noble like servanthood or peace? Dreams are the shapers of destiny. Perhaps all we have a right to dream for our children is that they grow into their truest selves. Perhaps all we can do is respect the sacred or the holy in our children and encourage them to discover their *own* dreams, rather than subtly or not-so-subtly imposing ours.

So, rather than asking what my dream is for my child, perhaps I should be asking what my dream is for *myself*?" Was there a star the night that I was born? Of course. One of the most important tasks of my life, then, is to discover what that star is *for me*. And as a parent and grandparent, one of my most important tasks is to encourage each child to discover his or her own star.

* * *

THEREIN HANGS A TAIL

About four inches of snow covered the the ground when my friend, Jim, and I set out for a long afternoon hike in the Berkshires in western Massachusetts. The third party on our little expedition was Tawny, Jim's handsome collie. Of the three of us, Tawny was the most exuberant and enthusiastic about this winter outing. Tail held high, he pranced and danced through the snow, dashing this way and that, dipping his snout from time to time into the snow to taste and feel the delight of the fluff and the cold. Before long, snow began to collect and form little ice balls on the fur between the pads of his feet. His discomfort became evident each time he lay down to gnaw at the caked snow and ice.

Jim helped him with this task, but it continued to plague Tawny, and the romping soon ceased. His tail was still high, and he led us enthusiastically along the trails, but bit by bit, his tail sagged lower. Eventually, instead of leading us, he was following us. As he tired of the discomfort, his spirit dwindled further, and his tail was now hanging straight down. Jim and I were also tiring, and whenever we stopped to catch our breath, Jim would spend a few moments with Tawny, stroking him and talking comfortingly to him. Instantly, Tawny would be reinvigorated. Up would come his tail, and for a while it was clear he was once again enjoying himself. Then the tail would again begin to droop, and he would fall further and further behind. We stopped. Jim patted, stroked, and comforted. Up would come the tail and the high spirits. To observe the instantaneous transformation caused by nothing more dramatic than a word and a touch of encouragement was remarkable

All this came back to me at a time in my writing when I was feeling most discouraged. I had been eagerly working on these reflections, energized and enthusiastic about what I was doing. Then the going got tough. My writing dried up. I was not clear how to proceed. The energy waned. Creativity was gone. Both my wife and my editor could see it happening. Then one day there came some needed words of encouragement from my wife, and on the same day an affirming e-mail from my editor. Incredibly, my energy returned, my spirits rose, and during the night creative ideas began to spin in my head. In the morning, I was back at the computer ready to go again, tail held high.

A word of encouragement and affirmation is such a simple thing, but it has the power to transform. Think today about the people whose paths will cross yours and whose delight in their journey could be greatly enhanced by a word from you. Think today about people who have done the same for you. Then go and do likewise!

*　*　*

THE FEELINGS I LIKE BEST

There are few blessings in this life any more satisfying than a cool drink on a hot day. Close behind, is a hot drink on a cold day. Both are blessings we take for granted in our little corner of the universe, but which cannot be assumed from one meal to the next in countless other places. Also high on my list of blessings is a time of rest following several days of bone tired weariness.

In my present stage of life, where I so seldom experience the bone weariness of hard work, I discover that I miss the experience of earned rest. I don't miss the weariness; I miss the rest that comes after the weariness. When I was a parish minister, there were days, weeks and months of what seemed like unrelenting demands upon my time and energy. Then came blessed weeks of vacation. I recall the unparalleled blessing of a vacation camp-site at Nickerson State Park on Cape Cod, the ecstasy of hot sun, warm sand, and refreshing ocean breezes, the sensuousness of bodies nearly bare -- my own, my wife's, and others unknown or less well-known to me -- and children's voices on the beach, and all tension draining away. All this was pure, intense, soul-satisfying pleasure. Much of what made those summer moments so memorable was not the moments themselves so much as the contrast they provided from the work-weariness that preceded them. The feeling I liked best was made possible only by the preceding feelings I liked least.

And then there is the universal cycle of separateness and togetherness, dissonance and harmony, distance and closeness, alienation and intimacy in relationships with those we love and care about the most. There is probably no more intense love-making than that which takes place when two souls have rediscovered their love after a period of distressing loneliness between them. The same is true in relationship to God, or to whomever or whatever one counts on for ultimate meaning in life. All the great spiritual men and women of the ages confirm that experiences of distancing are not aberrations or failures on our part. The feeling that accompanies return is most delicious when the separation has been most painful.

Too often I resent and distrust the loneliness, the weariness, the emptiness, thinking they will last forever. Better, I think, to experience them with trust, knowing that they are simply part of the process of living -- the process that finally lends itself to experiencing the feelings I like best.

* * *

GOOD DOG/BAD DOG SAM

Our son had a dog named Sam. A cross between a German Shepherd, a Doberman, and -- well, who-knows-what-else -- she was big, perky and playful. Often she greeted me at the door with her eyes bright and expectant, tail wagging, full of energy and ready for anything.

Sometimes, however, there was no greeting when I came in the door, no wagging tail, no big, bright, expectant eyes. Instead she would be standing in the hall pretending to be glad to see me, but failing miserably in the attempt. Her tail would be droopy, and something about her made her seem smaller than usual. Her eyes would be half closed, and I knew immediately that she had been doing something she shouldn't. I would go right away to the living room and put my hand on the couch where she was not allowed to go, and the couch would be *warm*! All this time she was watching me, her body was getting smaller and smaller and her eyes were becoming mere slits. I would get very stern, and say, "BAD DOG, B-A-A-A-D DOG!" And she would get smaller and smaller, and her eyes by now would be almost completely closed.

One day in a store I saw a mother and a little boy. The youngster had done something which upset his mother. In a loud voice she was berating him, saying, "You're BAD, BAD, BAD!" Right before my eyes, the little boy was getting smaller and smaller, and his eyes were full of tears. Bad, bad, bad. Just like Sam.

Sometimes after telling Sam how bad she was, I would get down on my knees and give her a hug and remind her that actually she was a very GOOD dog. And right before my eyes she would come back to life and get big again. Her eyes would no longer be little slits, and she would wag her tail, and look bright and expectant, full of energy and ready for anything.

I've seen it happen to little kids and big kids. I've seen it happen to grown-ups. I've seen it happen to *me*!

* * *

PEOPLE WHO HOLD ME UP

Back in the days when the wind for organs was created by pumps manned by young boys wanting to earn a few pennies, a famous organist was playing to a sell-out crowd in a huge auditorium. The audience was highly enthusiastic in its response. When the organist came back stage during an intermission, the young boy who had been pumping the wind for the organ said to the great musician, "Aren't we great?" The organist looked disdainfully at the youngster and said, "*We?* Who's *we?*" At the end of the intermission, the organist seated himself at the console, prepared himself for the opening chords, and with a great flourish hit the organ keys. Nothing happened, absolutely nothing. There was no wind to sound the mighty pipes. In the silence that followed came the little boy's voice: "*Now* who's we?"

There is a somewhat similar story in the book of *Exodus*. In a battle between the Israelites and the forces of Amalek, so the story goes, Moses, the leader of the Israelites, went up a hill overlooking the battle. Whenever Moses held up his hands, his forces prevailed. Whenever he lowered them, the enemy prevailed. Eventually Moses' arms got tired. So his companions located a large rock for Moses to sit on, and then Aaron on one side and Hur on the other held up Moses' arms so that his hands were steady until the sun went down, and the battle was won. (*Exodus* 17:8-13)

These two old stories remind me of how dependent I am upon the support of others -- my wife, for example, my daughters, my friends, my parishioners. Do they know how much their love, support, common sense and wisdom have meant to me? Do all these people know how essential they have been to me?

I need to stop periodically in my busy life to remind myself of all those who in one way or another have held up my arms. Who are they? Who would I be without them? And then I need to seek them out, *tell* them, and thank them!

* * *

VI. RESPONSE ABILITY

...Let me, dear God, be active
And seem to do right, whatever damned
        result.
Let me have some part in what goes on
Or I shall go mad!
                    Christopher Fry
                    in *The Sleep of Prisoners*

"What does the Lord require of you
but to do justice, and to love kindness,
and to walk humbly with your God?"
                    Micah 6:8

HUMAN SEISMOGRAPHS

Introducing Part VI

Given the amount of pain and suffering in the world, I sometimes think we are not so uncomfortable as we ought to be. I wonder whether our constant exposure to violence through television and news reports may not be creating moral callouses on our hearts.

With that in mind, I pricked up my ears when I heard about an experiment conducted back in the early sixties at the University of California at Davis. Two subjects were placed in separate sensory-deprivation rooms. Both were wired to measure heart rate, muscular activity, respiratory changes, and brain waves. One of them was subjected to random electric shocks. The other was to guess the precise moments when the shocks were being given. Neither subject could see or hear the other.

As reported by Michael Ventura and James Hillman, the results of the experiment were startling. The individual doing the guessing did not even come close to identifying the actual moments when the electric shocks were being given, but his polygraph reading showed significant physiological changes at those instants when the shocks were being administered.

If this experiment was valid, it suggests that even though at a conscious level we may not react to another's pain, at a biological level, the *body* reacts. I cannot vouch for the validity of the experiment, but quite apart from empirical evidence there seems to me to be some truth to the conclusion. I think, for example, of Somalia, Bosnia, Kosovo, Iraq, Rwanda, Haiti, and...and...and...and. I wonder what all the pain, suffering and violence in the world are doing to us at a fundamental biological level, all unbeknownst to us? What impact are they having on our collective unconscious, our psyches, our souls? Do our bodies as well as our minds eventually become numbed and calloused?

If the experiment at Davis is valid, perhaps we are more uncomfortable than we realize and pay a physiological, not to mention spiritual, price for the shocking events daily taking place all over the world.

In the words of Christopher Fry,

...there's not a skipping soul
On the loneliest goat-path who is not
Hugged into this, the human shambles.

111

And whatever happens on the farthest pitch
To the sand-man in the desert or the island
man in the sea,
Concerns us very soon.

Our willingness and ability to respond to the needs of others -- our response-ability -- is the only hope we have of being fully human. Without response-ability there cannot really be any peace or joy either in us or in the world. This will be the main thrust of these next few reflections.

* * *

ON SITTING LUCKY AND FAT

I give you fair warning. The poem below will unsettle you. Read it at your own risk.

Graceless we sit at grace, and the food gags
...in our mouths. Always we sit,
Lucky and fat, watching the hungry wait
And the poor die, our lost brothers. What nags
Are cold winds and our houses safe, while they
Perish without shelters, bodies in stacks
Across the world or bent like crooked sticks
Over garbage, finally faceless and gray.

Bewildered, caught between grief and anger
At what we do and what we do not do,
We hear the playgrounds where our children linger
Laughing, alive, dreaming. And then the view
Darkens. It is as if the birds were gone
And their songs lost in the indifferent sun.
                                    Arnold Kenseth
                                    In *Fiddler's Green*

When I open the newspaper or turn on the evening news, like the author of this poem I am bewildered, "caught between grief and anger and what we do and what we do not do."

The poem speaks for itself. No commentary is required. Perhaps all that is needed here is that I share it with you and urge you to read it again -- and then again -- lest, like the sun, we become indifferent, and thus, less than human.

The ability to respond -- our response ability -- is a God-given gift. It is an important part of what keeps us human. Poems like this one may be distressing. They are also essential for our individual and collective survival.

* * *

YOU DIDN'T DO ANYTHING AT ALL

The enormities of the times in which I have lived have forced me to take a part in resisting them.
Thomas Jefferson

As a teenager during World War II, I was appalled by atrocities committed by the Japanese against American captives. Then we learned about the so-called 'rape of Nanking,' where thousands of civilians -- men, women and children -- were the victims. Later, in seminary, a close friend of mine who had served in the infantry in Europe, confessed to me some atrocities he had personally both observed and committed, including the gang rape of a German woman and the deliberate terrorizing of a group of German children. In neither of these events did he step forward to prevent the cruelties.

Many years later I read a story told by a Japanese novelist about some gruesome medical experiments conducted by Japanese doctors using American prisoners as guinea pigs. The doctors rationalized that, since the prisoners were going to be killed anyway, experiments could be justified for the sake of gaining valuable medical knowledge. In his novel *The Sea and Poison*, Shusako Endo describes an intern named Suguro who suffers terrible pangs of conscience about performing these experiments. There came a day when Suguro, lacking the courage to refuse to participate, found himself unable to function in the operating room. Sickened and appalled by the atrocities being committed, he backs himself against the wall and watches. His conscience accuses him. He tries to excuse his passivity by telling himself, *"But I didn't do anything."* The author writes, *"...this plea seemed to reverberate within him, churning itself into a whirlpool devoid of meaning." "That's it!"* Suguro says to himself. *"You've hit it there! You didn't do anything at all....You're always...not doing anything at all."*

I think about times -- all too many of them -- when the circumstances of the moment called for protest or action and I was silent, doing nothing at all. As Suguro's conscience accused him, so my conscience accuses me. It's not that I have intentionally done anything immoral. Rather, in too many instances, I have not done anything at all. Might this not be, in fact, one of the ultimate immoralities?

You will understand, therefore, why this following 14th century anonymous English poem touches me:

> *Lord, you have called me,*
> *And I did only answer thee*
> *With words slow and sleepy:*
> *"Wait a while! Wait a little!"*
> *But while and while have no end,*
> *And wait a little is a long road.*

I ask myself what it might mean for my life if my answer were not so "slow and sleepy." What if instead of "Wait a while," I were to say, "Here I am, Lord. Send me!"

* * *

JELLY ON MY HANDS

In one of my favorite *Peanuts* cartoons, Linus becomes aware of his hands. He is carried away by a sense of the marvelous potential in those hands of his for doing great works and shaping destiny. Greatly impressed, he approaches Lucy, holds out his hands to her, and reflects on them. These hands may someday do great things. They might build great bridges; they might heal the sick; they might hit home runs; they might write soul-stirring books. These hands, Linus rhapsodizes, might even change the course of destiny. Lucy, unimpressed and cynical, quickly brings Linus down to earth. Glancing briefly at his hands, she says, "You've got jelly on them."

Any reader of history knows that *all* the hands that have changed the course of destiny have had jelly on them. They always will. That is the human condition. Nonetheless, to look only at the defects of church, nation, or self is to run the risk of becoming morbidly preoccupied with what ails us until we cannot be equally aware of the health, strength and power for good that are in us as well.

Linus was right. His hands -- our hands, collectively and individually -- are hands that may someday accomplish great things. They might even change the course of history. Lucy was also right -- those hands have jelly on them.

So -- would you rather be a Linus or a Lucy? Which holds the better vision of the way life is or might be? Which perspective encourages you toward the best that is in you? Which perspective discourages you by reminding you of the worst in you? Which stands the better chance of moving you, not in discouraging directions, but in hopeful ones?

Better yet, might it not be possible to be both Linus and Lucy at the same time? Might we not accept *both* sides of human nature -- the highest and the lowest? We know they are *both* present in us, in every human being and in most institutions. Never losing sight of our imperfections might we not still dare to dream of greatness?

I look at my hands. They *do* hold great possibilities. And they *do* have jelly on them.

* * *

NO MAN IS AN ISLAND

Does the name John Wayne Gacy mean anything to you? How about Theodore Bundy? Each has a story that should not be forgotten. Both men were found guilty of crimes that the courts determined were punishable by death, but it is neither their crimes nor their guilt that deserves to be remembered. What should not be forgotten is the way vast numbers of people responded to their scheduled executions, one in Illinois, the other in Florida.

In the case of John Wayne Gacy, large numbers of people treated his execution as an occasion for public celebration. As the date for execution drew near, a local radio station fanned the flames of this mood by broadcasting a daily countdown and advertising a celebratory parade to be held immediately after Gacy was declared dead. That is a story that should not be forgotten.

As for Theodore Bundy, as the hour approached for his electrocution, more than 2,000 people gathered outside the prison chanting, "Burn, Bundy, burn." T-shirts sporting Bundy slogans were sold. One of the best-sellers read, "I like my Ted well done." Another favorite read, "Roast in peace." That, too, is a story that should not be forgotten.

As macabre as those two stories are, and as repulsed as I

115

am by them, I cannot plead "not guilty." When I pass an accident on the highway, something in me is drawn to the horror of it. Even if it is clear to me that my help is not needed, I take my foot off the accelerator and try to get a good look. When two hockey players go head-to-head with their fists or their sticks, as disgusted as I am by such antics, with a surge of excitement I leap to my feet along with everyone else. In days of public hangings, large crowds showed up to watch, to joke, to cheer, to be horrified. It was entertainment. What I dare not forget is that I, too, have within me a strange fascination with death and violence. Fights on hockey rinks and accidents on highways may not be in the same league as the sick displays of public celebration at executions, but do not both stem from the same roots?

John Donne reminded us that *"No man is an island....any man's death diminishes me, because I am involved in mankind...."* That, too, is something I do not want to forget.

* * *

NUMBNESS AS A CRIME

In an old paperback called *The Whitman Reader,* there is a fascinating collection of poems and journal entries by Walt Whitman. Particularly gripping are some of his writings about the Civil War. These entries bring me face to face with some of the almost unimaginable atrocities of that war. I say unimaginable, but that is not quite true because almost daily I am assailed by accounts of similar atrocities and horrors taking place all over the world. People sometimes ask, "What is this world coming to?" Walt Whitman reminds us that this is not what we are *coming* to, but what has always been, and not only among less 'civilized' people than ourselves. Here, for example, is one of Whitman's journal entries:

> *The releas'd prisoners of war are now coming up from the southern prisons. I have seen a number of them. The sight is worse than any sight of battle-fields, or any collection of wounded, even the bloodiest. There was, (as a sample,) one large boat load, of several hundreds, brought about the 25th, to Annapolis; and out of the whole number only*

three individuals were able to walk from the boat.
The rest were carried ashore and laid down in one
place or another. Can those be men -- those little
livid brown, ash-streak'd, monkey-looking dwarfs?
Are they really not mummied, dwindled corpses?
They lay there, most of them, quite still, but with a
horrible look in their eyes and skinny lips (often
with not enough flesh on the lips to cover their
teeth.) Probably no more appalling sight was ever
seen on this earth. (There are deeds, crimes, that
may be forgiven; but this is not among them. It
steeps its perpetrators in blackest, escapeless,
endless damnation. Over 50,000 have been
compell'd to die the death of starvation -- reader, did
you ever try to realize what starvation actually is? --
in those prisons - and in a land of plenty.) An
indescribable meanness, tyranny, aggravating
course of insults, almost incredible -- was evidently
the rule of treatment through all the southern
military prisons. The dead there are not to be pitied
as much as some of the living that come from there
-- if they can be call'd living -- many of them are
mentally imbecile, and will never recuperate.

Whitman called this a crime that may not be forgiven.
Might it be true that an even greater crime, even less forgivable,
is the numbness that seeps into our souls with the constant
barrage of horror stories that invades our living rooms and dens
on a daily basis? Numbness, after all, immunizes us from *feeling*
the horrors of which that we humans are capable. Numbness,
finally, dehumanizes us, and therefore is a crime in itself. Who
among us can plead, "Not guilty?"

* * *

LIVE FREE OR DIE

"Live Free or Die"-- that is the patriotic slogan which appears on my New Hampshire license plates. An alternative, and possibly more relevant, slogan for New Hampshire appeared on a car with South Carolina plates. Parked at a White Mountains trailhead on a chilly late-October day, the bumper sticker read, "Live, Freeze and Die."

Licenses and bumper stickers notwithstanding, history reminds us that ideals and realities often contradict one another. For example, one of the principal aims of the original settlers of Concord, Massachusetts, as expressed in their charter, was to "win the Indians...to the knowledge and obedience of the only true God and Savior of mankind and the Christian faith." What that really meant was that they intended to transform the natives and make them more like the English.

When persuasion failed to make good Englishmen out of the Indians, those early colonial authorities tried enforcement. They did this by drawing up orders in 1646 regarding the behavior of the Indians -- note, the Indians, not the Englishmen!

1) Indians were to be fined for drinking -- 20 shillings.
2) They were to observe the Lord's Day -- 20 shillings fine for failure to do so.
3) They were to cease and desist from picking lice -- fine, 1 shilling per louse.
4) They were to stop greasing themselves -- fine, 1 shilling per default.
5) They were to pray in their wigwams and say grace before and after meals.
6) They were forbidden to play their former native sports.
7) They were not to commit adultery -- punishable by death.
8) They were not to engage in 'howling' as an expression of grief.

Those are just a few of the twenty-nine orders designed to make the Indians more like the English.

Concord, of course, was no worse than most early colonial towns in this regard. My point is simply that even to the present day, in the name of freedom and religion we humans are prone to abuse other humans. I think, for example, of our culture's prohibitions on homosexuals and the Church's historic attitudes toward the Jews. Such contradictions between the ideals we proclaim and the actions we live by are as appalling now as they were in 1646.

* * *

SAVED BY A HEAVY LOAD

An ancient wisdom held by many religions is that we should share one another's burdens. The message is so familiar that it may seem a bit ho-hum. Even though I believe this ancient wisdom is true and that I should seek to live by it, I confess there are times when the last thing I want to do is share someone else's burden -- my own burdens often feel like quite enough.

One day recently when I was feeling particularly resistant to sharing burdens, I came across a story about a small tribe of Indians who lived long ago in Mississippi. Their village, we are told, was next to a shallow, but extremely swift, river, whose current was so strong that anyone attempting to cross was in serious danger of being swept downstream and drowned. There came a day when a hostile tribe attacked them and they were soon fighting with their backs to the river-which-no-one-could-cross. Having no alternative, they gathered the youngest and oldest members of the tribe, and the strong ones placed the weaker ones on their shoulders and waded into the river. To their amazement, the weight of their fellow tribesmen on their shoulders kept them from losing their footing, so that they were able to cross the river and escape without harm. The strong were saved only when they took upon themselves the burden of another.

I do not know whether this account is historically accurate, but the point it makes is true.

* * *

HANG IN THERE

Driving through Northfield, Massachusetts one day, I was brought up short by the sight of a man hanging by his finger tips from a second-story window. I braked hard and backed up to see what was going on. The ladder on which he had been standing had fallen off to one side and was leaning at a

119

precarious angle just beyond reach of his feet. Something clearly had to be done and done fast. Only then did I realize that this desperate-looking fellow was not a real live man, but a dummy. The jokester who had hung him there had accomplished his purpose, which was to get me to stop at his nursery and possibly buy some flowers or plants.

Over and over when the going was hard, people have said to me, 'Hang in there!' I wonder how many times I have said those words as well. If the man dangling from the window ledge had been a real person, I probably would have yelled, 'Hang in there!' as I ran for help. I would have intended those simple words as encouragement, a good and necessary thing. But that poor fellow hanging from a window did not need encouragement nearly so much as he needed someone to replace the ladder. Until that happened, 'Hang in there' might at least have given him hope that help was on its way.

The next time I find myself saying to someone, 'Hang in there!' I hope I will also have the good sense to look for a ladder to put under his or her feet.

* * *

THE POWER OF A THING

I was fifty-six years old -- old enough to know better -- but that summer I fell in love. Like many summer love affairs, this one was brief, but passionate and all-consuming. In my eyes the object of my affection was irresistibly beautiful. Her lines and curves were exquisite, a delight to behold, and a delight to my touch. Having found her, I returned to see her several times. I took pictures of her so I would have something to remember her by in the long winter days and nights. I dreamed about her by day and by night. Deep inside, however, I knew I couldn't have her. She was far beyond my means. Furthermore, I didn't have a convenient place to moor her. My passion, as you may have guessed by now, was a sailboat. If ever there was love at first sight, this was it, and I became obsessed.

This experience was a vivid reminder to me of the power of a thing. I had come face to face with covetousness before, and here it was again, fresh and all-consuming. I define covetousness as a craving, a longing for something or someone. Covetousness is wanting gone out of control. Almost everyone knows the feeling. When we were young, perhaps we craved a bicycle, a pony or a dog. Today we might yearn for a Nikon camera, a new car, an RV, or the house we have always dreamed of. The longing gets under our skin, distorts our perspective and threatens to take over our life. Our judgment becomes clouded. Coveting can literally become an illness of mind, heart and spirit.

Rumi once said, **"I have become suspicious of what I want."** Therefore, when I find myself obsessed by something I want, the best advice I have learned to give myself is to be suspicious of my wanting, to wait a while -- usually a *long* while. More often than not, with time and suspicion, some perspective and sanity take over. I also find it helpful to remind myself that the best things in life aren't things.

* * *

WHEN DOES NIGHT CHANGE TO DAY?

The pupils gather around a Rabbi, who speaks to them as follows: "I have a question for you. How can one tell the moment when night changes to day?"

The students ponder the question. One says, "Perhaps it is when there is enough light that one can see if the animal in the distance is a dog or a cat."

The Rabbi says, "No, that's not the answer."

They reflect some more, and one offers, "Perhaps it is when there is enough light that when looking out one sees a tree and can tell whether it is a fig or a peach."

"No," responds the Rabbi, "that's not it either."

The class considers the question a while longer. Not wanting to risk another wrong answer, they are silent. The Rabbi then says, "My friends, the time when night changes to day is when you look into the face of a man or woman -- *any* man or woman -- and you can see that he is your brother and she is your sister. Until that time comes, it will always be night."

* * *

WHAT SHALL WE SING?

When people mention the Gulf War, what comes immediately to my mind is how few casualties we --Americans, that is -- suffered. How soon I forget. Over 100,000 Iraqis dead, 72,000 homeless, 2,000,000 Kurdish refugees trying to flee to Turkey, and thousands more who were turned away -- to go where? When the Gulf War ended, thousands of bodies lay strewn across the Middle East desert. Many of them were soldiers. Countless others were women and children.

The Bible tells us, "The earth is the Lord's and the fullness thereof, the world and *all who dwell therein.*" That means that every war on this planet, no matter how justified, is a civil war -- brother and sister against brother and sister. It also means that the loss of any child of God, of whatever age, shape, size, color, or nationality, must be an anguish to God, just as the loss of one of our own children is such an unspeakable grief to us.

In the year 297 A.D., Rabbi Johannan told a story which illustrates this. He describes the destruction of the Egyptians in the Red Sea when they were pursuing the Israelites to capture them and bring them back into slavery. The Israelites were clearly the good guys and the Egyptians were the bad guys. So, writes the rabbi, when the bad guys got drowned, the ministering angels wanted to sing a hymn of praise at their destruction. But God said, "No! My Egyptian children lie drowned in the sea; how can you sing?"

Annie Dillard tells us that the famous author, Nikos Kazantzakis, had a canary which he kept in a cage. In his living room he had a globe. On occasion, Kazantzakis would free the canary from its cage and it would perch on top of the globe and sing. I imagine myself as that canary sitting on top of the globe and asking, 'What song shall I sing?' I decide to sing the words written in the *Acts of the Apostles,* 17:22-28: *"The God who created the world and everything in it, and who is Lord of heaven and earth...is the universal giver of life and breath and all else...we are all God's offspring."* That, it seems to me, must be our theme song, and whatever else we sing should be in harmony with that.

*   *   *

WHAT WORRIES YOU?

My mother was only sixty-nine when she died. Unfortunately, her spirit had begun to die several years earlier as she progressively withdrew from her former capacity for compassion. The horizons of her world had shrunk. Something in her had died before her body did. In contrast, my step-mother died when she was eighty-three. In spite of a body which had begun to give out several years earlier with deafness, gimpy legs, and what I suppose was osteoporosis --though the label wasn't much used in those days -- she continued to expand her horizons and never lost her compassion for the world and those about her where she lived. When she was lying in her hospital bed on the verge of death -- or so we thought -- one of my sisters asked her, late one evening, "Jo, is there anything you're feeling worried about?" She reflected for a moment, then replied, "I'm worried about the world." Her horizons had not narrowed. The hospital room and the small town of Oberlin, Ohio, where she lived, never defined the limits of her concern. She was worried about the world, Even on the edge of death, she did not look on coolly as others suffered.

I titled these reflections, "When I Open My Window." Jo, I think, never needed to open hers --it had never been closed.

* * *

THE TWO FACES OF CHRISTMAS

The year was 1937. I was eleven years old. The Japanese had invaded China, and because the area where we lived was considered dangerous for foreigners, we could not return to our home in Shantung province. For Christmas that year, we were therefore living temporarily in someone else's house in the North China city of Tientsin -- now Tianjin.

In spite of unsettled circumstances and meager resources, my parents, gave us a full-scale Christmas. We had a tree, hung decorations on it, and under it were gifts. I say there were gifts, but I remember only one. Under the tree, with no wrapping to hide it, was the shiniest, most beautiful pair of ice skates I had ever seen. I still see them as clearly as if that Christmas were yesterday. I was thrilled beyond words. No other gift I received that Christmas or any Christmas since excited me more than that pair of skates.

123

These were not ice skates as modern kids know them. They had no boots attached. They consisted of a simple shiny metal platform with an even shinier blade which clamped onto one's street shoes -- nothing for ankle support, nothing for warmth -- just a blade flimsily attached to my shoes.

That afternoon, in a biting cold and dusty wind, my father took me to a nearby pond. There was so much grit and dirt on the bumpy ice that I could hardly see the surface and there was precious little to slip or glide on. But I *skated*! It was glorious. It didn't even matter that the clamps kept slipping off the soles of my shoes.

A little Chinese boy, perhaps five or six years old, spotted us, and came to the edge of the pond, watching enviously. Dad, as was his habit, soon engaged him in conversation. Eventually, knowing that this area had been bombed heavily by the Japanese, he asked the boy about the war. "What was it like?" What I recall -- and I remember this almost as vividly as I remember those shiny new skates under the tree -- was the stark terror in the little fellow's eyes, and the quaver in his voice as he described the bombing of his little village on the outskirts of the city.

Those two memories are clearer to me than any other childhood Christmas memories -- the shiny new skates and the small boy's terror. Not a Christmas goes by without those two vividly contrasting recollections coming unbidden to my mind. It seems to me still that these are always the two faces of Christmas, just as they have been from the very beginning. Both those faces of Christmas are in the Bible:

> *When they saw the star, they rejoiced exceedingly....Then opening their treasures, they offered him gifts, gold and frankincense and myrrh. (Matthew 2:11)*

> *Then Herod...in a furious rage...sent and killed all the male children in...all that region who were two years old or under. (Matthew 2:16)*

So -- I remember.

* * *

THE CHRISTMAS EVE VISITOR

On a bitter-cold Christmas Eve, our church was full for the late service. Just as we were finishing, a young man collapsed in the balcony. An ambulance was called and I followed it to the Emergency Room at the nearby hospital. As I stood with his parents at the young man's bedside, a nurse beckoned me out to the waiting room. Two teenagers, eyes wide, informed me breathlessly that there was a homeless woman back at the church who desperately needed help. Having been reassured the young man was going to be all right, I returned to the church -- reluctantly I confess, for it was getting late and my family was waiting for me at home for some special Christmas Eve time together. This was *not* how I had planned to spend my Christmas Eve.

I found the homeless woman at the church. As the teenagers had surmised, she was in serious trouble. She was ill, she had no place to stay, there was no money for lodging that night nor for food on Christmas Day, and she apparently had no family to whom she could turn.

What to do? There were compelling reasons why I did not want to invite her back to my own home, including the fact that our son was seriously ill, and we had reason to suspect this could well be our last Christmas with him. I felt trapped in a moral and spiritual dilemma. How, on Christmas Eve, of all times, do you tell a homeless person there is no room in the inn? I was up against the classic experience Jesus describes in the parable of the last judgment: *"I was hungry, and you would not feed me, thirsty, but you would not give me drink; I was a stranger, but you would not welcome me into your own home...I was sick and you would not take care of me."* In the story, the people defended themselves, saying, *"When did we ever see you hungry or thirsty or a stranger or sick and we would not help you?"* And the answer came, *"I tell you, whenever you did it not to one of the least of these, you did it not to me."* (Matthew 25:31-40)

I do not believe that this Christmas Eve visitor was literally Jesus Christ in disguise, but she might as well have been. I was thoroughly shaken by my reluctance to get involved. Where was my compassion? What did this do to my image of myself as a caring person? She may not have been Jesus, but through her I was confronted by the Christ. What a bummer, I thought, to have to meet the Christ on Christmas Eve!

I did find her a room that night and food for Christmas day. In the weeks and months that followed, she got the medical and psychiatric care she needed. The important part of the story, however, was not so much what happened to her as what happened to me.

I think of experiences like that -- and we all have them in one form or another -- as God's elbow in my ribs. I do not believe for one moment that God deliberately set me up that night. I do not believe God caused that woman to become mentally ill, or that God caused her to be homeless, or that God caused her own family to reject her and refuse to help. I do not believe God caused her to walk into my life that night. I *do* believe that the creative and loving power and energy of God were at work in that otherwise tragic situation, that there was a divine Grace at work in it, and that through that Grace God propelled me into a painful reassessment of my own compassion and commitment. I was jolted into questioning what it means to be a Christian -- or, for that matter, simply to be a mature and caring human being. In that sense, this lost and lonely Christmas Eve visitor was God's elbow in my ribs, and thus became an indelible part of what Christmas now means to me.

* * *

I WILL NOT CLOSE MY WINDOW

Epilogue

I live in what my friend, Arnold Kenseth, calls an antiseptic village -- *"... a white church, clean neighbors, cushy lawns."* That is not to say that all is as idyllic here as it appears on the surface. Yes, there is some poverty, though one must look harder to find it here than in most places. Yes, there are some abusive husbands and wives, but their sounds do not echo in my hallways or filter through the walls of adjacent apartments. Yes, there are drugs, and yes, there is some violent crime, but this I see mainly in the newspaper, rather than in my front yard. In short, though not quite so antiseptic as it appears, my hometown, compared to much of the rest of the world, is a haven of tranquility and ease. I confess I like it that way. All the more important, therefore, that I open my window wide enough to see, hear and feel what is happening not only in my own 'village,' and within my own heart and soul, but also beyond the boundaries of the places where I live.

Therefore, as I come to the end of these reflections, I make myself some promises:

- I will keep my window open to my yearning for a closer relationship with God.
- I will keep my window open to all the beauty and goodness that surround me.
- I will keep my window open during the dark times that come to me whenever I find myself walking through the valley of the shadow.
- I will keep my window open to what it means for me and those around me to grow older.
- I will keep my window open to deepening my relationships with friends and loved ones.
- I will keep my window open to the cries of the world and its unending needs.

In short, I will continue to live here in my 'antiseptic village,' lucky, fat, laughing, alive, and dreaming, but I will open my window wide and keep it open to the sounds that drift in from the world -- the inner world and the outer, the lovely and the unlovely, the light and the dark, the living and the dying, the wounding and the healing. Some of those sounds will come from very far away. Others will come from as close as the silent, secret places of my soul. Whatever the sounds and whatever their source, I will *not* close my window.

Finally, I invite you to consider what kinds of promises you might make to yourself and to those you love.

*   *   *

CREDITS AND PERMISSIONS

I. YEARNING FOR FAITH

Page 11 - Christopher Fry, *The Sleep of Prisoners* (Oxford University Press, NY, 1951), p. 48. Reprinted by permission of the Oxford University Press.

Page 14 - Jay Parini, *Robert Frost: A Life* (Henry Holt and Company, © by Jay Parini, 1999), p. 19. Reprinted by permission of Henry Holt & Co., LLC.

Page 15 - Abraham Heschel, *I Asked for Wonder: A Spiritual Anthology,* ed. Samuel H. Dresner (Crossroad Publishing Co., 1983), page 17. Reprinted by permission of Crossroad Publishing Co.

Page 20 - Martin E. Marty, *A Cry of Absence: Reflections for the Winter of The Heart* (HarperCollins Publishers, 1983), page 2. Reprinted by permission of HarperCollins Publishing, Inc.

Page 20 - Abraham Heschel, *I Asked for Wonder: A Spiritual Anthology,* ed. Samuel H. Dresner (Crossroad Publishing Co., 1983), page 5. Reprinted by permission of Crossroad Publishing Co.

Page 24 - Margaret Donaldson, *Human Minds: an Exploration* (Copyright ©1992 by Margaret Donaldson.) Used by permission of Viking Penguin, a division of Penguin Putnam Inc.), page 80.

Page 25 - Abraham Heschel, *I Asked for Wonder: A Spiritual Anthology,* ed. Samuel H. Dresner (Crossroad Publishing Co, 1983), page 19. Reprinted by permission of Crossroad Publishing Co.

Page 28 - Parker J. Palmer, *Let Your Life Speak* (Jossey-Bass, Inc. San Francisco, CA, 2000) page 7. Reprinted by permission of a subsidiary of John Wiley & Sons, Inc.

Page 32 - J. Barrie Shepherd, *Praying the Psalms* (Westminster Press, Philadelphia, PA, 1987), page 56. Reproduced from *Praying the Psalms,* by J. Barrie Shepherd, ©1987 The Westminster Press. Used by permission of Westminster John Knox Press.

Page 35 - Abraham Heschel, *I Asked for Wonder: A Spiritual Anthology,* ed. Samuel H. Dresner (Crossroad Publishing Co, 1983), p. 24. Reprinted by permission of Crossroad Publishing Co.

Page 35 - Frederick Buechner, *The Faces of Jesus* (A Stearn/Harper & Row Book, 1989), page 148. Reprinted by permission of the publisher.

Page 36 - Andrew Canale, *Beyond Depression: a Practical Guide for Healing Despair* (Element, Rockport, MA, 1992. ©Andrew Canale, 1992), p. 121. Reprinted by permission of Andrew Canale.

Page 37 - Barbara Brown Taylor, *"A Manner of Speaking,"* (Copyright 2000 Christian Century Foundation.) Reprinted by permission from the 9/27-1`0/4, 2000, issue of the Christian Century. Subscriptions $42/yr. (36 issues), from P.O. Box 378, Mt. Morris, IL 61054. 1-800-208-4097.

Page 38 - Scott Elledge, *E.B.White: a Biography* (W.W.Norton & Co., Inc. Copyright ©1984), p. 309 and 315. Reprinted by permission of W.W.Norton & Co., Inc.

Page 41 - John Shea, *The Hour of the Unexpected* (RCI Enterprises, Inc. Allen, TX, 1992), Reprinted by permission of the publisher.

Page 43 - Wendell Berry, *A Timbered Choir, the Sabbath Poems 1979-1997* (Copyright ©1998 by Wendell Berry) page 18. Reprinted by permission of Counterpoint Press, a member of Perseus Books, L.L.C.

II. ON BEING MORE FULLY ALIVE

Page 49 - Matthew Fox, *Original Blessing,* (Bear and Co., Santa Fe, NM, 1983), page 112-113. Reprinted by permission of Matthew Fox.

Page 51 - Annie Dillard, *Pilgrim at Tinker Creek,* (Bantam Books, 1974), pages 9, 102, and 276. Reprinted by permission of HarperCollins Publishers.

Page 53 - Pat Conroy, *Beach Music* (Doubleday, NY, 1995), p. 495. Reprinted by permission of Doubleday, a division of Random House.

Page 56 - Abraham Heschel *(I Asked for Wonder, a Spiritual Anthology,* ed. Samuel Dresner (Crossroad Publishing Co., 1983) pages vii and 3. Reprinted by permission of Crossroad Publishing Co.

Page 56 - John Steinbeck, *East of Eden,* (©1952 by John Steinbeck, ©renewed 1980 by Elaine Steinbeck, John Steinbeck IV, and Thom Steinbeck. Viking Press, 1986), page 17. Used by permission of Viking Penguin, a division of Penguin Putnam, Inc.

Page 58 - Arnold Kenseth, *Sabbaths, Sacraments and Seasons: A Collection of Meditations, Prayers and Canticles*, (The Pilgrim Press, Philadelphia, 1969), page 95. ©1969. Reprinted by permission of The Pilgrim Press.

Page 59 - Sam Keen, *Hymns to an Unknown God,* (Bantam Books, NY, 1994), pages 262 and 275. Reprinted by permission of Bantam Books, a division of Random House.

III. WALKING THROUGH THE VALLEY OF THE SHADOW

Page 66 - Archibald MacLeish, *J.B.* (Houghton-Mifflin, N.Y. Copyright 1956, 1957, 1958, renewed in 1986 by William H. MacLeish and Mary H. Grimm), p. 11. Reprinted by permission of the Houghton-Mifflin Company.

Page 69 - Antonio Machado, reprinted from *Times Alone: Selected Poems of Antonio Machado*, translated by Robert Bly, (Wesleyan University Press, Middletown, CT, 1983. Copyright 1983 Robert Bly.) Used with his permission.

Page 70 - Rolf Jacobsen, reprinted from *News of the Universe*, edited by Robert Bly, (Sierra Club Books, San Francisco, 1980. Copyright 1980 Robert Bly.) Used with his permission.

Page 70 - Juan Ramon Jimenez, reprinted from *Lorca and Jimenez: Selected Poems,* edited by Robert Bly, (Beacon Press, Boston, 1973. Copyright 1973 Robert Bly.) Used with his permission.

Page 71 - Frederick Buechner, *The Alphabet of Grace* (The Seabury Press, NY, 3rd printing, 1981. Copyright, 1970), pp. 7-8. Reprinted by permission of the Domestic and Foreign Missionary Society of the Protestant Episcopal Church.

Page 73 - David Comstock in a letter to Jane Gilbert Keith. Reprinted by permission of the author and the recipient.

Page 74 - Theodore Loder, from an Easter sermon. Reprinted by permission of the author.

IV. GROWING OLDER

Page 79 - May Sarton, *Collected Poems, 1930-1993* (W.W.Norton & Co., Inc. Copyright ©1993, 1998, 1984, 1974.) Reprinted by permission of W.W. Norton & Co., Inc.

Page 81 - Ted Loder, *Wrestling With the Light* (Innisfree Press, Philadelphia, PA, 1991), pp. 95-96. Reprinted by permission of the Innisfree Press

Page 82 - Doris Grumbach, *Extra Innings: a Memoir* (W.W.Norton & Co, Inc., 1993), p. 185. Copyright t© 1993 by Doris Grumbach. Reprinted by permission of W.W. Norton & Co.,Inc.

Page 87 - Lois Palches, *"A Light-hearted Death Wish."* Used with permission of the estate of Lois and Peter Palches

V. RELATIONSHIPS

Page 95 - Peter Riggs, in a letter to the Shansi Memorial Committee, Oberlin College, Oberlin, Ohio. Used by permission of Peter Riggs.

Page 98 - Thich Nhat Hanh, *Peace Is Every Step*, ed. Arnold Kotler (Bantam Books, NY, 1991), page 77. Reprinted by permission of Bantam Books, a division of Random House.

Page 100 - Henri Nouwen, *The Return of the Prodigal Son* (Doubleday, NY,

1992), p. 121. Reprinted by permission of Doubleday, a division of Random House.

Page 102 - Elizabeth O'Connor, *Cry Pain, Cry Hope* (Word Books, Waco, TX, 1987), p. 138. Every reasonable effort has been made to locate a publisher and/or owner of the copyright, but without success.

Page 102 -Pablo Casals, *Joys and Sorrows.* Reprinted with permission of Simon & Schuster from JOYS AND SORROWS: Reflections by Pablo Casals as Told to Albert E. Kahn. Copyright © 1970 by Albert E. Kahn. Copyright renewed © 1998 by Harriet W. Kahn.

VI. RESPONSE-ABILITY

Page 109 - Christopher Fry, *The Sleep of Prisoners* (Oxford University Press, NY, 1951), p. 41. Reprinted by permission of the Oxford University Press

Page 111 - Christopher Fry, *The Sleep of Prisoners* (Oxford University Press, NY, 1951), p. 45. Reprinted by permission of the Oxford University Press.

Page 112 - Arnold Kenseth, *Fiddler's Green* (Windhover Press, Amherst, MA, 1999), p. 28. Reprinted by permission of Arnold Kenseth.

Page 113 - Shusako Endo, *The Sea and Poison* (Copyright © 1958 by Bungai Shunju Co. Ltd., Tokyo, 1972 by Peter Owen). Reprinted by permission of New Directions Publishing Corp.

Page 116 - Maxwell Geismar, *The Whitman Reader* (Pocket Books, Inc. a division of Simon & Shuster, 1955), p. 322. Reprinted with the permission of Simon & Shuster from *The Whitman Reader*. Copyright ©1955 by Maxwell Geismar.

Unless otherwise noted, all quotations from Scripture are from the New Revised Standard Version, Copyright ©1989 by the Division of Christian Education of the National Council of the Churches of Christ in the USA. Used by permission. All rights reserved.

All possible care has been taken to fully acknowledge the ownership and use of the quoted materials in this book. If any mistakes or omissions have occurred, they will be corrected in subsequent editions, provided notification is sent to the author.

ABOUT THE AUTHOR

Chandler Gilbert, known to most as Tuck, was born on the *Tuck Wo*, a British river steamer on the Yangtze River in China. Most of his childhood was spent in North China where his parents were Congregational missionaries. Growing tensions between the United States and Japan forced their evacuation from China in 1940. Tuck then attended high school in Newton, Massachusetts, received a Bachelor of Arts degree from Oberlin College in 1947, a Master of Divinity degree from Yale Divinity School in 1951, and a Doctor of Ministry degree in pastoral care and counseling from Andover Newton Theological School in 1977.

An ordained minister in the United Church of Christ, his first parish was Central Park Congregational Church, a new-start church, in Toledo, Ohio. For three years he then served as Associate Minister at First Congregational Church of Akron, Ohio. This was followed by thirteen years as Senior Minister of First Congregational Church in Westfield, Massachusetts, and eighteen years as Senior Minister at Trinitarian Congregational Church in Concord, Massachusetts.

In 1988, he and his wife, Bobbie, moved to Jaffrey, New Hampshire, where they provide a retreat space called The Creative Pause, serving clergy and/or their partners. For over twenty years, Bobbie and he also led communication and enrichment workshops for married couples. Both are certified Leaders and Trainers for the Association of Couples for Marriage Enrichment.

Over the years, Tuck has enjoyed camping, hiking New England mountains and hills, playing tennis, sailing, and canoeing both white water and flat water. Currently his extra-curricular activities center on walking, reading, writing, photography, grandchildren, and singing in the Monadnock Chorus.

ORDERING INFORMATION

Please order directly from:
Chandler W. Gilbert
23 Parsons Lane
Jaffrey, NH 03452
Phone: 603-532-4366
E-mail:tbgilbert@monad.net

Single Copy of Book: $12.50
(If shipping is required, add $2.50)

Single Copy of 90-minute audio cassette with
selected readings from the book: $7.50
(If shipping is required, add $2.50)

Special combination offer:
Book & Tape: $18.00
(If shipping is required, add $2.00)

If ordering multiple copies to one address:
1-5 copies: S & H is $2.50
6-10 copies, S & H is $4.00

Orders will be sent Book Rate and may be sent as gifts
to a different address.

MAKE CHECK PAYABLE TO
CHANDLER W. GILBERT

PLEASE PRINT ALL NAMES AND ADDRESSES